With his extensive experienc
as an interfaith adviser in the
ethnic city that is contempor.
better-placed person than Dr
grounded wisdom for churches and Christians navigating multifaith Britain today. Deeply rooted in scripture, Smith communicates a compelling vision and call for Christians to engage practically in the rapidly changing world around them. His gift is to empower others through making Christian missional presence and engagement in multireligious contexts accessible and exciting. Packed with hands-on tips, this book will be used by churches with gratitude as they seek to pursue the historic vocation to be the body of Christ for all people.

Mark Poulson
Secretary for Inter-Religious Affairs to the Archbishop of Canterbury and National Inter-Religious Affairs Adviser for the Church of England

As a British Gujarati Christ follower, this book has helped heal some of the tender spots on my journey to Jesus. It has also made me realise the genuine need of maintaining and nurturing family ties in order to love with genuine Christ-like love. As an evangelical Christian, I am challenged to admit, face and dismantle my own rhetoric and dare to explore again what it means to live as a vibrant Christian.

Usha Reifsnider
Programme Coordinator with the South Asian Forum at Evangelical Alliance

Vibrant Christianity in Multifaith Britain is easily accessible and personally challenging to anyone who cares about lived faith and lively community in contemporary society. Andrew Smith's extensive first-hand knowledge of world faiths and passion for Chrisitian witness have been shaped into essential tools for renewed presence and engagement among those of all faiths and none. Here the disciple of Jesus Christ seeking to serve will find new confidence for participating in the mission of God in the power of the Holy Spirit and so fulfil his kingdom purpose.

Rt Revd David Urquhart
Bishop of Birmingham

The Bible Reading Fellowship
15 The Chambers, Vineyard
Abingdon OX14 3FE
brf.org.uk

The Bible Reading Fellowship (BRF) is a Registered Charity (233280)

ISBN 978 0 85746 571 9
First published 2018
10 9 8 7 6 5 4 3 2 1 0
All rights reserved

Acknowledgements
Unless otherwise stated, scripture quotations are taken from The Holy Bible, New
International Version (Anglicised edition) copyright © 1979, 1984, 2011 by Biblica.
Used by permission of Hodder & Stoughton Publishers, a Hachette UK company.
All rights reserved. 'NIV' is a registered trademark of Biblica. UK trademark number
1448790.

Every effort has been made to trace and contact copyright owners for material used
in this resource. We apologise for any inadvertent omissions or errors, and would
ask those concerned to contact us so that full acknowledgement can be made in the
future.

A catalogue record for this book is available from the British Library

Printed and bound by CPI Group (UK) Ltd, Croydon CR0 4YY

Vibrant Christianity in Multifaith Britain

Equipping the church for a faithful
engagement with people of different faiths

Andrew Smith

Acknowledgements

This book has been possible only because of the help and encouragement of so many friends who over the years have taught me and encouraged me in this ministry. I would like especially to thank Emlyn Williams and Bishop David Urquhart, who, as employers at different stages in my life, have given me the freedom to explore and develop new ways of working. I'd also like to thank, and honour, the team at The Feast, who have been brave enough to take my ideas and run with them, teaching me so much more in the process.

For the many friends of different faiths who have encouraged me by their friendship and insights and have patiently answered questions and requests.

Also to the many Christians who have informed my thinking and challenged my ideas and to those of many faiths who were willing to read through this manuscript and make honest and helpful comments.

Finally, none of this ministry would have been possible without the support and inspiration of my very patient wife, Sarah, and my boys, Jack and Matthew, who have put up with my being out a lot and being either frustrated or excited about what's going on, and who have spent many hours listening to me as I tell them all about what I'm up to.

Contents

Introduction 7

1 What do we think of other faiths? 11

2 A different question 21

3 Them and us? 39

4 The great commission 49

5 Doing dialogue 67

6 Being peacemakers 79

7 Cultural issues 89

8 The church: reaching out and welcoming in 107

Notes 119

Introduction

Back in 1978, when I was 11 years old, I used to love watching *Top of the Pops* on a Thursday evening. It was a highlight of the week's TV schedule, which, let's face it, was meagre fare back then. Although I enjoyed the programme, and am now able to watch endless repeats, many of the acts were pretty forgettable. But occasionally one would stand out from the crowd. One such band was Boney M, who suddenly appeared wearing shiny silver jumpsuits and singing a song that I didn't understand but which my parents assured me was from the Bible, with its lyrics about rivers of Babylon and singing the Lord's song. I never really liked the song and thought Boney M looked a bit embarrassing, but it had one of those tunes that gets stuck in your head, irritatingly catchy and unforgettable. One of the lines that I always remembered was 'How shall we sing the Lord's song in a strange land?' Many years later I discovered that the lyrics were indeed from the Bible and came from Psalm 137, referring to the people of Israel's exile in Babylon. They were taken to a 'strange land' where people spoke a different language, ate different food and worshipped foreign gods, and when it was demanded that the they sing their worship songs, the Israelites found that they couldn't do it. Being in such a strange place meant that the old songs didn't make sense; indeed, how could they sing the Lord's songs in such a strange country?

Over the past couple of decades I've met with many Christians who have asked how they can make sense of their faith in a country that is home to an increasing number of people from different faith traditions. For many people who grew up in the UK before 2000, the world has changed dramatically, religion is rarely out of the news, usually for all the wrong reasons, and Britain is increasingly described as a multifaith society. Other faiths, particularly Islam, are much more visible in politics, education, popular culture and the news. Consequently, when people are discussing how to share their faith or what place Christianity has in society many of the old certainties have gone; we are no longer the one dominant religious voice in a sea of unbelief, but one of many – and not always the loudest. For many Christians this raises numerous questions about how they express their faith, through either words or actions. In other words, how do we now sing the Lord's song in this strange land?

This is a journey that I went on back in the mid 1990s in Birmingham. I'd grown up in a Christian family, attending a big evangelical church in the south of England, but until I was about 28 I'd never actually met someone who was a member of a different faith. At school in the 1980s, pretty much everyone rejected the idea of God or religion and there was a general view that all religion was slowly dying out. If Christians had ever taught me anything about other religions, it was that they were inferior to Christianity and that there was no spirituality in them; rather, they were purely ritualistic. Our job as Christians was to tell people of other faiths about Jesus, because then they would be spiritually fulfilled when they became Christians. This made sense to me, until I actually met some Muslims. I met some people who loved being Muslim, talked about faith in spiritual rather than ritualistic terms and articulated very clearly how they found spiritual fulfilment within Islam. Obviously a young Christian turning up and preaching simplistic sermons at them was not what they were looking for. Consequently, like so many others, I started to ask the question in one form or other: 'How do I sing the Lord's song in this strange land?'

Having only ever mixed with secular people, I'd never had to work out how I related to or understood the faith of others. In many ways it challenged the simplistic notions of faith and Christianity that I had. Here were people who thought religion was a good thing and weren't expecting it to die out; they believed in God, prayed, read scriptures, went to a place of worship, wanted to tell others about their faith and thought that their faith should inform the way they lived. It all seemed really close, yet vastly different, to the Christian faith that I experienced. One consequence was that I asked big questions of the Christian faith. Was Jesus 'the way and the truth and the life?' What was it that made Christianity unique? How did the message of the gospel relate to people who seemed to be quite godly people yet denied that Jesus was the Son of God?

These are some of the questions that this book will seek to answer. Since that time, I have got to know and become friends with people of many different faiths, including Muslims, Sikhs, Hindus, Buddhists and Jews. I have spoken to large numbers of Christians trying to make sense of the changing world and wanting to 'sing the Lord's song' in ways that make sense to people of different faiths, yet not sure what words to use or how to get started. I've also come to realise that there are many different ways in which Christians answer these questions, often disagreeing quite strongly about what we should be doing and how we should go about doing it.

Although there are now many people engaging with those of other faiths in creative and interesting ways, I firmly believe that this is a task for the whole church and not just a few interfaith experts or specialised cross-cultural missioners. Having spent over 20 years trying to share my faith and be a witness to the good news of Jesus with people of different faiths, I can honestly say that it's been rewarding, fun, frustrating, disappointing and enriching in equal measure (and this is true of my work with churches over that time as well). My faith in Christ has been deepened; I've made some really good friends and I've also changed the way I read the Bible. I find myself asking, 'What would my Sikh friend think if she read this passage?' or 'How would this sound to a Buddhist?'

I've also gone back to scripture time and again to interrogate it for myself, to try to discern what God might be saying to me in the context of multifaith issues or in relation to specific questions or challenges. Sometimes I've discovered passages that I haven't noticed before, but more often I've rediscovered more well-known texts or found God speaking to me in new ways through them. One such text is Luke 6:31, 'Do to others as you would have them do to you.' This saying has been so commonly referred to, often as 'The Golden Rule', that I think we've neglected to consider what it would mean to obey it. When considering what it means to live a vibrant Christian life among people of different faiths, I've discovered that this verse is deeply challenging and really helpful. Do I want people to listen to me talk about my faith? If the answer is yes, then I need to do the same to them and listen to them talk about their faith. Do I want people to visit my church? If so, then I need to be willing to visit their gurdwara or mosque. Not only did the verse challenge me to think differently when I started this ministry, it also reassured me that it's okay to visit a Buddhist vihara or listen to a Hindu explain their faith. Jesus wants me to treat them as I want to be treated.

I've also been aware of how little I know. I have a simple rule that's stood me in good stead for 20 years and that I'll pass on to you. All I do is smile and ask. That's it really. Whether I want to know why a Hindu temple has a deity that I haven't seen before or why a Muslim friend is fasting, all I do is smile and ask. So far no one's been offended or upset; usually it leads to a conversation that goes in all sorts of directions. So, if you remember one thing from this book, use this as a way of getting to know and understand different faiths: just smile and ask.

1

What do we think of other faiths?

A spiritual scale?

A young man thinks he's got everything: money, power, youthful good looks, but still feels uneasy about his life. All those big questions about who he is, what will happen when he dies and what the purpose of life is keep haunting him. Then one day he hears that the rabbi that everyone's talking about, famous as a great preacher and miracle worker, is in town. So, the young man rushes off and to his surprise gets right up close to him. He blurts out the first thing that comes to mind. 'Good teacher,' he calls out, 'what must I do to receive eternal life?' He's hoping for a resolution to this most perplexing question, but when the answer comes it's not what he's looking for. Although he insists that he keeps God's laws, this new preacher takes him by surprise. 'Go,' he calmly says, 'and sell all your possessions, give the money to the poor, then come and follow me.' The young man is stunned. When he said 'eternal life', he meant in the future, after he'd died; he wasn't expecting it to affect the way he uses his money now. So, he has only one option: he turns and walks away.

That story from Matthew 19:16–26 highlights many people's starting point when thinking about how Christians relate to people of other faiths. The questions they have are all about what people must do to receive eternal life. But usually this is code for 'who is going to be in heaven?' Typically, these questions are about whether people of different faiths will get into heaven, and what about people of different faiths who have never heard the gospel? For some people, it's clear that no one except Christians will be in heaven; others are less certain, especially if they've started to meet people of other faiths who are living good lives and ones centred on prayer and worship.

These questions also apply to people of no faith, but often they only get asked in reference to encountering people of different faiths. Why is that? Why are we more concerned about these questions when relating to people of faith when they actually apply in all sorts of situations? Before we go on to look at how we might respond to questions of salvation, I want to look at why people tend to get more concerned about them when it comes to thinking about engaging with other religions.

A few years ago I came up with a theory of how many Christians view the world, which I call 'the spiritual scale'. I have described it before, but wanted to expand upon the idea here.[1] I want to show how, I think, it permeates and affects much of the way we view the world, and therefore our engagement with it, and particularly how it affects the way we relate to people of different faiths. The spiritual scale looks something like this:

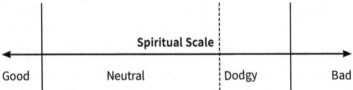

What do I mean by 'spiritual'? In this instance, I mean things that are in line with God's will and enable us to grow to be more holy. There will be many different interpretations of what God's will is in different situations, and different definitions of 'spiritual'. The idea of the scale is not a method of discerning God's will or defining spirituality, but a way in which, I think, people relate to the world. When we look at the world in this way, some things are considered spiritually good (for example, churches) and other things are considered spiritually bad (which often include other faiths), but much of life (such as shopping or holidays) is seen as just spiritually neutral. The consequence of viewing the world like this is that we can become uncritical of things that we might consider spiritually good, wary of or hostile to things that we think are spiritually bad, and ignore the impact on us of things that we think are spiritually neutral.

Why do I think people view the world in this way? Because I often meet people who live and talk like this, even though they are usually unaware that that is what they are doing. For example, I often take groups of Christians to visit mosques, gurdwaras or mandirs and, on occasion, people ask if they can pray for spiritual protection before they go in, and many tell me that they were praying for that during the visit. If that's what people need to do in order to feel secure then I'm happy for them to do that, although in my experience no one has ever been spiritually attacked or led into sin during these visits, even if they have found them uncomfortable or challenging. In fact, some pray so hard during the visit I think it might be the best prayer time they've had for a while.

However, after the visit people go off to their usual lives of shopping, watching TV and going online. As they do this, no doubt like many of us they will worry about the clothes they wear or the food they eat despite being commanded not to by Jesus (Matthew 6:25); they will be tempted to be greedy or to look at inappropriate images or to gamble money they can ill afford and so on. But I have never heard anyone suggest that we pray for protection before we go shopping or log on to the Internet or switch on the TV. Why? Because places of worship of other faiths are considered to be spiritually bad, whereas shopping, the Internet and TV are considered neutral or at worst a bit dodgy. By viewing the world as a spiritual scale, they are being uncritical of things considered neutral and critical of things considered bad despite not necessarily having any evidence for this point of view.

Many years ago I was meeting with some Christians to talk about whether we wanted to set up a dialogue meeting with some Muslims.

The idea ground to a halt when someone asked whether we could legitimately work with Muslims on a dialogue programme when really all we wanted to do was convert them. I found this fascinating, as I was fairly sure that if we had met to talk about working with the police on tackling anti-social behaviour in our area, no one would have asked that question about the police. It was one of the first times I realised that Christians were viewing people in very different ways: some as spiritually bad and in need of conversion; others as spiritually neutral, so there was no need to consider sharing the gospel with them.

The final conversation I heard that convinced me that people view the world like this was between two people who had both just finished at a mission college. One had got a job in the local authority and was telling us his concerns about his boss, as he had just found out she was a witch. 'Does that make any difference?' his friend asked. 'Yes,' he replied, 'I'll have to start praying for her *now*.' For some reason, she wasn't worthy of prayer before but now he knew she was a witch he felt compelled to pray. In his mind, she had moved from neutral to bad and so now needed prayer.

At this point I need to say a few things about this spiritual scale. The main point I want to make is that I think it is wrong! I don't think the world can or should be viewed like this or that different religions, organisations or beliefs can be simply categorised as 'spiritually good' or 'spiritually bad'. Despite the fact that viewing the world like this is almost ubiquitous, it's a dangerous way of doing so. What I want to show is why it's so problematic and contrary to biblical teaching.

First, it means we prejudge situations, missing opportunities or challenges they may present. When I'm talking to churches about letting their young people come to a Christian–Muslim youth event I'm running, there are often questions about whether the Muslims will attempt to convert the Christians and many churches are wary about getting involved. Yet when I've run events where Christian and secular young people are mixing, no one asks these questions. This is a classic case of living by the spiritual scale and, therefore, being blind to the reality of life. When I ask people whether they know any Christians who have joined another faith, usually one or two hands go up. If I then ask if they know any Christians who have just drifted away and become secular, virtually every hand in the room goes up. Yet we are happier for young people to mix with a secular group than a Muslim one. People are leaving the church not, on the whole, to convert to Islam but to drift off into secularism, but because many Christians have a spiritual scale that suggests that other faiths are spiritually bad and secularism is spiritually neutral, they are wary of one and not the other despite evidence that suggests a more complex picture.

I think for Christians to see the world as a spiritual scale is wrong, as I don't think God sees the world like this. While there may be a very few things that can be considered totally bad or totally good from a spiritual perspective, most things are far more complex, with elements that are spiritually good – that is, in line with God's will – and others that are far removed from what God wants. In the Old Testament we read of Nebuchadnezzar, who wreaked such havoc on the people of Judah, besieging and attacking Jerusalem and carrying them into exile in Babylon, where they faced his fiery furnace (Daniel 3). Yet far from being considered as spiritually bad and therefore totally outside God's will, he is frequently described in the book of Jeremiah as God's servant and eventually comes to 'praise and exalt and glorify the King of heaven' (Daniel 4:37). Even someone as despotic as Nebuchadnezzar cannot be placed on a spiritual scale and written off as spiritually bad or neutral. Like the rest of us, his character and temperament were far more complex.

Today we can see similar examples in the world around us. A clothes shop might work to make sure its garments are made by people working in good conditions (which would make God happy) while still encouraging us to buy clothes we don't need (not what God might want). My Muslim friends will deny that Jesus is the Son of

God, but they can be exceptionally patient and generous and self-controlled with me, things that God wants. Similarly, churches might be delivering wonderful worship, programmes for young people and creative evangelism, while being uncaring about the elderly or LGBT members of the congregation.

If we're honest, this complexity of being both close to and far away from what God wants describes most of us most of the time. The task we have when engaging with the world, and particularly the world of different faiths, is to keep questioning whether we are using a spiritual scale to determine what we think about a situation, a person, a place or an entire faith. Then we need to ask not whether they are good, bad or neutral, but what we can find in them that is spiritually good. What is there that pleases God that I can celebrate and what displeases God that I need to question or challenge? This can be true for Christians of all traditions. Some Christians I know from the liberal tradition still view the world as a spiritual scale; it's just that what's considered good, neutral or bad is different. But it still results in the same problematic way of engaging with the world. Finally, what I don't think we can do is consider some things to be neutral; all systems, structures or people contain elements that are good and bad, but not neutral.

Who is going to heaven?

I started this chapter by suggesting that for many Christians this question is their starting point. It's a question that has been written about by a huge number of scholars, and three basic approaches to this have been described. They are usually called exclusivism, inclusivism and pluralism. I'm going to give a very brief overview, but if you want to read more, some good authors to look at would be Harold Netland and John Hick.[2]

Exclusivism

This is the belief that Christianity as revealed in the Bible is the only true faith and that accepting Jesus Christ as Lord is the only way to salvation. Other faiths might be morally good, but they contain nothing that will save people from their sins. Heaven is saved for those who believe and trust in Jesus Christ as Lord, and some maintain that only those who consciously commit their lives to Jesus, usually through a prescribed prayer, are saved. This was the orthodox teaching of the church for many centuries and is still a standpoint adopted by many Christians today. While this view, which offers no salvation for people who haven't heard the gospel, might seem harsh to some, exclusivist theologians emphasise God's love and justice – if decisions seem unfair to us, it is because of our limited view and we can trust God's infinite wisdom to get them right.

Pluralism

Many Christians have found the exclusivist standpoint difficult when meeting devout, godly people from different faiths, or when thinking of those who have never heard the gospel. Would they really be condemned to an eternity of punishment through no fault of their own? How does this sit with a God of love? Pluralism describes different faiths as different ways in which people have sought to worship and respond to the one true God, sometimes described as the 'Ultimate Real'. The faiths are true for those who believe them but are not exclusively true, so there is the possibility of salvation in all faiths. Pluralists want to affirm the beliefs and practices of all faiths but also to suggest that not all faiths are equal (that's relativism). For example, a religion that practised human sacrifice would not be placed on the same level as those that condemn such practices.

Inclusivism

As the popularity of pluralism grew in the latter half of the 20th century, many Christians who were unhappy with the judgmental basis of exclusivism were also unhappy with pluralism's denial of the exclusive truth claims made by, and about, Jesus Christ in the Bible. The God who loves the whole world (John 3:16) is also the God who sent his Son Jesus as 'the way and the truth and the life' (John 14:6). There seems to be both a wideness to God's love and an exclusivity to it through Jesus. Inclusivist theologians started to look at how the scriptures describe God at work beyond the church or the people of Israel and to argue that one can see God's Holy Spirit at work in the world and that people might be responding to the prompting of the Holy Spirit. Ultimately, however, it is through the death and resurrection of Jesus that people are saved, whether they acknowledge that or not. Inclusivism argues that if people of different faiths are in heaven (and the presumption is that many will be), it will be because God in his wisdom has judged them to be people living according to his will from the best of their knowledge, and that Jesus' blood was shed for all, so covered them as well. It's almost as if Jesus stands before God the Father and says, 'They're with me.'

Clearly, a brief paragraph on each position does not do justice to the thinking that has gone into these three perspectives, but the aim of this book is not to re-work those arguments. I want to acknowledge that this has been the framework for Christian engagement with other faiths for many years, but also to suggest that for many Christians trying to live out their faith in normal life this isn't always a helpful model. It tends to focus solely on the question of who is saved – in other words, who is going to be in heaven – rather than on other questions, particularly in relation to how we live alongside people of other faiths now.

Each of the standpoints can reinforce the idea of a spiritual scale by placing those who agree with it as spiritually good and those in opposition as spiritually bad. Because the model doesn't deal with other questions about society (such as poverty, injustice and gender issues), those questions are left out of the discussion and so can easily be relegated to the status of spiritually neutral or irrelevant. It's almost as if religion is all about entry tickets to heaven and our task is to discern who's got the tickets and how we can offer those tickets to others. Like the rich young ruler we thought about at the start of this chapter, we need to learn that following Jesus isn't just about entry tickets to heaven but is also about life now; for him eternal life included giving all he had to the poor. For us eternal life might include befriending someone of another faith. Asking who is going to be in heaven might be an important question, but it certainly isn't the only question we need to ask, nor is it the only question Jesus ever asked us to consider.

For some Christians, moving from a spiritual scale to a more flexible approach where we try to discern positives and negatives in all situations and people is challenging. We can feel uncomfortable moving away from the certainty of 'we're right and they're wrong'. Being willing to recognise our own frailties and failings and then also to acknowledge the good and positive in others is a big ask for many people. Perhaps one of the biggest challenges in encountering people of other faiths is the realisation that we are not living the life Jesus has called us to. Seeing the example of others should, in the words of a Muslim friend of mine, 'spur us on into acts of righteousness' – drawing us closer to Jesus, not further away.

So, who is going to heaven? I actually think that question needs quite a lot of unpacking, which is what I'm going to do over the next few chapters. Also, there are other questions the Bible poses that are just as important and that shed light on this issue and impact the way we behave towards people of different faiths.

Questions

- Think about the way you view different aspects of your life or people you meet. Do you put them on a spiritual scale?

- Draw out the scale and write down where you often place the things you do or the situations or people you encounter. Now try to look at each of those things and identify the good to be encouraged or the bad to be challenged in each of them. Where did you put other faiths? Has this affected the way you see them?

- What are the questions you have when you think about encountering people of different faiths? What might Jesus be challenging you to ask?

2

A different question

The great commands

'You ask him, you're the most experienced.' The group of religious leaders stood in a huddle planning their next move. The troublesome preacher was back in town stirring up the crowds and running rings around them in their disputes. Debating in public was what they were good at, developing intricate and clever arguments to explore the meaning of God's word. They did this regularly and were used to the cut and thrust of debate. But this new preacher, he was something else. He seemed to look at everything from a different angle, wrong-footing them at almost every turn, and the crowd in the market loved it. In the end one of them, deemed to be the expert in interpreting the law, came forward, cleared his throat and asked his question: 'Teacher, which is the greatest commandment?'

If 'Who gets to heaven?' isn't the main question I want to focus on in this book, then what should that be? In the scene imagined above, based on Matthew 22:34–40, Jesus is asked this famous question and, in his inimitable style, he manages to answer by suggesting two commandments. Jesus makes it clear that the greatest commandment is to 'Love the Lord your God with all your heart and with all your soul and with all your mind' (v. 37). He then goes on to add the second, which is to 'Love your neighbour as yourself' (v. 39). He says that all the law and prophets are summed up in these two commands. However, I want to suggest that not only are these important commands for us in our relationships with people of different faiths, but there is something very significant in the fact that they always go together. We are commanded to love God *and* our neighbour, not one or the other.

This was nothing new in biblical teaching. Jesus would have heard and read the Torah, including passages such as Deuteronomy 10:12, where Moses asks the people of Israel, 'What does the Lord your God ask of you?' In the answer that follows he says, 'And you are to love those who are foreigners, for you yourselves were foreigners in Egypt' (v. 19). The command is not to tolerate or put up with the foreigners but to love them. Of course, if they were foreigners they wouldn't have been Jewish; they would have been from a different country with different food, language and even gods. But the very next verse is significant, because having told them to love the foreigner Moses then says, 'Fear the Lord your God and serve him. Hold fast to him and take your oaths in his name.' In other words, love God. Loving the foreigner who worships other gods does not mean giving up on holding fast to and loving God.

This was the idea that Jesus was building on when he instructed his hearers to obey both of these commands *at the same time*. We are called to love our neighbour of any faith and at the same time to be faithful in loving God. It is the obeying of both of these commands that is the crucial challenge for the church today. While we can theorise as to who may or may not be in heaven, we have been given the commands to love God and love our neighbour.

It would be much easier if these commands were separated, and often the church has behaved as if they were. A cursory look at the history of the church in Europe (and probably elsewhere as well) leads us to conclude that too often the attitude of the church has been, 'We love God properly and if you don't love God our way we will ridicule, denounce, excommunicate or even kill you.' The command to love God has been thought to have been obeyed, but it has not been constantly checked against the command to love our neighbour. On the other hand, I have met Christians committed to interfaith work who are intensely focused on loving their neighbours of different faiths, but when I mention my belief in Jesus as the Son of God they complain that I'm causing tensions and difficulties by raising beliefs others don't subscribe to. They are obeying the comand to love their neighbour but at the expense of holding fast to God. Somehow we have to find a way constantly to obey both of these commands.

There is another reason why they go together, which helps us obey them both; that is that they actually build on each other. The more we are confident in our love for God, the greater love we can have for our neighbours as we see them as made in the image of God and loved by him. If you look back at the Deuteronomy passage you'll see that in verse 18 Moses says that God loves the foreigner. Before commanding the people of Israel to love he states God's love for them. Loving our neighbours of different faiths is not a burden or duty; it is a chance for us to join in with God's love for them. He is not sending us to do something he doesn't want to do, but inviting us to join in with what he is already doing. It's worth reminding ourselves every now and then just how much God loves the Muslims, Sikhs, Hindus and others living near us or appearing on the news. However much we might learn to love our neighbour, it will never be as much as God loves them.

Over the years that I've got to know people of different faiths and tried to love them, I've found that the result has been a growing of my love for God. Some people think that if we mix with people of different faiths then we'll get confused and drift away from God, whereas the experience of many people, including myself, is that learning to love our neighbours of different faiths strengthens our faith and deepens our love for God. The commands are linked.

A friend of mine who is a leader in the Sikh community often says that if we want to do interfaith well, then we should do faith well. We should make sure people are rooted in their own faith so that they can contribute well in interfaith settings. He is not looking for encounters with other faiths to be confusing or to weaken people's faiths; instead he challenges leaders of all faiths to teach their congregations well.

There are a couple more things to notice about these commands; first, the command is to *love* our neighbour. We often pride ourselves on being a tolerant society or having respect for people different from ourselves. However, that is not what Jesus commands us to do; we are commanded to love, which is far more demanding and challenging. Tolerance is fine as far as it goes, but in truth we tolerate things we don't like. I often travel on buses and sometimes find myself sat next to someone who hasn't washed as well or as recently as I would like. Maybe I should say something to them, but I don't; I tolerate them. It's better than being rude or violent, but it isn't love. Respect might be seen as better than tolerance, as it's not just about putting up with things we don't like. But respect can be very passive. I can have tremendous respect for people of different faiths, including those I've never met, but it might not change the way I live. It's good, but it's not love.

The challenge we're faced with is to love our neighbours, and particularly in this context to love our neighbours of different faiths. Love is neither putting up with something we don't like nor passive. Genuine love is a positive emotion and leads to action. I remember once being told by some Christians that they loved the Muslims in their town. 'That's great,' I said. 'So if I go to the mosque and chat to them they'll talk about how much you love them and what you've done for them, will they?' 'Well, no,' the people from the church replied, 'we've never actually met them.' I think they were describing respect. Genuine love means that we do something for the people we claim to love.

Suddenly we start to see that asking 'How can we love our neighbours of different faiths?' might be a more radical and life-changing question than 'Who's going to be in heaven?', because when we ask what it means to love the answer will involve our *doing* something. Loving our neighbours means getting to know them, their names, their hopes, dreams and fears. It means looking out for them and standing alongside them when they are having a tough time. It would be so much easier if Jesus had said we should tolerate or respect our neighbours, but he didn't. He commanded us to love.

Love, certainly in the Bible, means taking the initiative, reaching out even when we aren't loved back. In the same way that God doesn't send us to do this but invites us to join him, so he doesn't ask us to be active while he is passive. The greatest example we have of active love is God sending Jesus to live among us, to teach, to suffer, to die and to be raised to life. This is done not out of exasperation, tolerance or respect but out of love (Romans 5:8).

I hope you're getting the idea now that loving our neighbour is a key concept in how we relate to people of other faiths, and that we have to do that while continuing to love God faithfully. When we love in this way we start to treat people not as a threat, or a project or a target for evangelism, but as people. We stop trying to work out their position on a spiritual scale and then to move them from that. We recognise their God-given humanity, which includes much that is good and that can build us up as well as the issues in their lives that need challenging or healing. People sometimes ask me how they can start a conversation with their Hindu friends. I say, 'Start by asking "How are you?"' Treat them as people, be interested in them, love them!' It also occurs to me that if you love someone you're usually pleased to see them. It would be pretty odd to love someone but be annoyed or displeased by their presence. So, this raises the question – are we pleased to see people of other faiths living in our neighbourhoods? Do we love them enough to think, 'Oh good, I'm glad you live here'?

The final point I want to make about these commands is that they are unconditional. We don't love God only when he answers our prayers in the ways we want him to; neither do we set limits on our love for our neighbours. It would be so much easier if Jesus had said, 'Love your neighbour *if* they are like you, or *if* they want to become a Christian, or *if* they don't play their music too loud or park inconsiderately.' It's a natural human reaction to want to add 'if' to this command, but Jesus didn't and neither can we. It's very easy when we are passionate about our faith to have a hidden agenda in our relationships with people of other faiths, to claim that our friendship is genuine when really our motive is for them to become Christians. While we may long for that for all of our neighbours, unconditional love starts and goes on loving without any motives other than to love.

Loving our neighbours in this way can be really challenging, but it opens up new ways of being faithful Christians with people of different faiths. We can find all sorts of ways to express our love, which might include sharing the gospel or sharing a meal. It might mean standing with them if they face abuse or accepting an invitation to a Diwali party or Eid celebration. It also becomes a lifelong and life-changing experience. Our love for our neighbours doesn't end if they reject the gospel or show little interest in what we believe. It should be genuine and unconditional and always rooted in our love for God. Loving a Buddhist doesn't mean you have to convert to Buddhism. The challenge we face is to keep asking how we can love God more and how we can love our neighbours of other faiths more. Those, I think, are the questions we should be asking as we work out what it means to discover a vibrant Christianity in a multifaith society.

Love as an ethical code

There's a famous passage in the Bible that explores in some depth what God's love looks like and what it means for us to live according to that way. However, for some reason this passage tends to get read only at weddings, which makes me wonder if that's the only time churches think we love people. It also reduces a challenging, provocative passage about how we live to a romantic poem that one might find in a wedding card. I'm talking, of course, about 1 Corinthians 13 and particularly verses 4–7, where Paul lays out in simple terms what an enduring godly love looks like in practice.

There are times when our relationships with or attitudes towards people of other faiths are tested. We might hear of how Christians are being persecuted in other parts of the world or see packed gurdwaras near to half-empty churches. It might seem to us that other faiths get funding or attention that we think Christians miss out on, or feel that Christianity is sidelined in favour of other religions in public life. It's at times like these that I think this passage really speaks to us and gives us the spiritual resources to respond. It challenges us not to be envious of the growth of other faiths and not to keep a record of the wrongs others do even when these are against our brothers and sisters. It forbids us from being proud of what Christians do or being easily angered by the bad behaviour of others.

Studying this passage in the light of how we feel about and relate to people of different faiths would be a useful task for a church; that is, to use it not just as a romantic poem but as an ethical code for life. It forces us to address the good and bad in ourselves and others and to behave in a new way when we encounter challenges and difficulties. It's another way scripture debunks the idea of a spiritual scale. This passage doesn't set up the fully-loving ones against an unloving other, but rather is an inspiration and challenge to us to see what loving in a godly way would actually look like.

Loving and serving

While I place great store on Jesus' commands to love God and love our neighbour (as you may have noticed), I'm also aware that this is not the only thing he said or did that can help us work out how we should be expressing our faith among friends of different faiths. Another key concept that we find in the scriptures is that of the servant. Jesus came taking the nature of a servant (Philippians 2:7), behaved as a servant in washing his disciples' feet (John 13:12–17) and instructed his disciples to be servants (Mark 10:43). Paul regularly described himself as a servant of God (e.g. 2 Corinthians 6:4) and of the church (e.g. 2 Corinthians 4:5). Being a servant is part of what it means to be a follower of Jesus, but what does it mean to be a servant among neighbours of different faiths? Bishop James Jones makes the point that, for Jesus, serving was not a means to an end but an end in itself.[3] For Jesus, serving was without an agenda or conditions, just like his love and the love he commands from us. There are many churches and Christians who have developed really good ministries among people of different faiths based on serving. These include language classes, carer and toddler groups, and refugee and asylum work. I've had the privilege to visit many of these over the years and seen some excellent examples of Christians serving, often with the selfless, agenda-free approach that James Jones argues is Christ-like serving.

However, sometimes I wonder if we confuse being a servant with being a doctor. Let me explain. A doctor is someone who can assess what's wrong with you and, you hope, prescribe a medical treatment to affect a cure. A doctor has the resources, knowledge and skills to make your life better. The doctor starts by asking what's wrong and then works out the cure. They might give you options and involve you in discussing the treatment, but they retain a certain amount of power and a professional distance from their patients; we go to the doctor only when we need them. The servant, however, is in a very different position. A servant starts by asking what you want and then goes about making it happen. The servant has very little control: they might be asked to fetch a drink, go to the shops and clean the windows or whatever their master wants. The servant is at the beck and call of the master, paid to be available for whatever the master wants. Being a servant is hard work, unglamorous and not nearly as rewarding as being a doctor.

In life, we need both doctors and servants; both are valuable but they are different. To choose to be a servant is to choose hard work and loss of status, is to choose a life that constantly asks of others, 'What do you want me to do?' When we explore the image of the servant in this way we can see that, again, Jesus calls us to a challenging encounter with people of other faiths. He doesn't say we shouldn't sometimes be like a doctor; if we have the skills and resources that can help people who are economically disadvantaged or being exploited or harassed, then we should use them. But we should also consider what it would mean to live as servants of others, to ask Muslims, Sikhs or Buddhists, 'What can we do for you?' We can be quite good at saying, 'We know what's good for you.' But if we ask, 'What can we do for you?' we might be surprised or deeply challenged at the answers. We might be asked to speak out against Islamophobia or racism, to support their planning application for a new temple or to support their request to have different faiths taught in the local school. Being a servant is challenging and not always comfortable.

Fortunately, we can turn to scripture to help us work through the question of what it would mean to be a servant. A good place to start is in 1 Kings 8:22–54, where King Solomon is dedicating the new temple he has built and offering an amazing prayer. Throughout his prayer Solomon asks God to hear the prayers of those who turn to the temple, and it's the kind of people you'd expect: the sick, the hungry, those fearful of war. But then in verses 41–44 we get this passage:

> As for the foreigner who does not belong to your people Israel but has come from a distant land because of your name – for they will hear of your great name and your mighty hand and your outstretched arm – when they come and pray towards this temple, then hear from heaven, your dwelling-place. Do whatever the foreigner asks of you, so that all the peoples of the earth may know your name and fear you, as do your own people Israel, and may know that this house I have built bears your Name.

Solomon includes the foreigners in his prayer and asks God to do whatever the foreigner asks. Notice that he doesn't say 'if they've converted' or 'if they ask for something that we agree with', but just give them what they ask for. Yes, they've heard of God and come towards his temple but what they believed or thought as they prayed is not questioned or dictated. This is the attitude of a servant right there in his prayer of dedication for the temple.

The example of Jesus

I mentioned above that for Jesus, serving was an end in itself, not a means to an end. Whether he was washing his disciples' feet (John 13:3–11) or feeding a crowd of 5,000 (Matthew 14:13–21), Jesus serves without demanding a response or looking for results. This has a profound message for us in our ministry among people of different faiths. It's very easy to get into a mentality that serving should be a means to an end. We run language courses *so that* people will come to church, or a toddler group *so that* we can share our faith with the carers.

But when Jesus taught about serving in Matthew 25 he made it clear that serving is the key, not the result. In the parable of the sheep and the goats, the 'sheep' are called to receive eternal life just because they had served. What the people they served made of their activities we are not told – because that's not the point, the point is that they served. I think too often we read that parable not as Jesus told it but by adding in our own conditions:

- I was hungry and you gave me something to eat – so I came to church.
- I was thirsty and you gave me something to drink – so I joined a discipleship group.
- I was a stranger and you invited me in – now I'm a Christian.
- I needed clothes and you clothed me – so I started to help with Sunday school.

- I was ill and you looked after me – now I'm on the pastoral team at church.
- I was in prison and you came to visit me – I'm now an evangelist.

OK, so it's slightly tongue in cheek, and sometimes these things do happen, but my point is that often we want to serve as a means to an end. The joy of this parable is that Jesus lifts that burden from us. He just wants us to serve, and if no one comes to church as a result, that isn't failure. Our task is to serve. What people make of our serving is between them and God.

Similarly, when Jesus fed the 5,000 it's interesting to ask how many of the crowd (which, of course, was actually way more than 5,000 as that figure included only the men) became followers of Jesus as a result of the encounter. The great news is that we don't know: some may have, they all may have or none may have, but we don't know. If we needed to I'm certain that God would have inspired one of the Gospel writers to include it. I say it is great news because once again it lifts a burden of expectation from us; the example is of service, not of results.

Clearly there are examples of Jesus encountering someone and their going on to follow Jesus, such as the two blind men whom Jesus heals in Matthew 20:29–34, but the Gospels are overwhelmingly silent on how people responded to Jesus following a healing or other act of service.

I think it's really important that we hear this news that our calling is to love our neighbour and then to serve them unconditionally as an end in itself. I meet many Christians who feel deflated by their ministry with people of different faiths. Many have been given high expectations of seeing large numbers of converts, but after several years the reality is that, if they have seen any conversions, the numbers are really small. With this mindset, ministry can become a burden grinding us down and leaving us believing we have failed God.

I've been there myself. I came into this work under the impression that if I loved my Muslim neighbours, served them and told them about Jesus, then many would become Christians. After several years of toiling away with no 'results', I felt as if I was failing. I used to get asked by fellow Christians, 'Any converts yet?' – often with a look in their eye which suggested that what they really meant was, 'Are we winning?' I'd then make some jokey comment about the fact that I'd been going for only seven or eight years so was just getting started, but inside I felt like a failure. It was only through studying passages like these that I began to see that not every activity Jesus did ended with numbers of converts, but that didn't mean he was a failure.

I also started to think about what life 'to the full' (John 10:10) meant in this context and began to see that maybe God was doing more than I realised, just not what I thought he should be doing! I began to ask God to show me what he had been doing rather than ask, rather grumpily, why he hadn't done what I thought he should. Once I started doing this I began to see amazing things that God was doing: conversations and friendships that were growing and deepening; opportunities to serve Muslims or share my faith that had been closed just a couple of years before. I started to see that what I needed to worry about was whether I loved God and my Muslim neighbours more than I had done and whether I was serving them to the best of my ability. This was what I needed to be concerned about; my success was not based on the responses of others but on my willingness to be obedient and faithful in the way I followed Jesus.

This sense of failure reflects a wider problem. Many Christians from evangelical churches have come to the conclusion that an activity is only ever really Christian if it includes an opportunity for people to make a conscious response to the gospel; in other words, did people become Christians? We'll look in more detail at the issue of evangelism and conversion in Chapter 3, and particularly why people are wary of or opposed to conversion. But the reality is that many people from different faiths are quite happy to meet with Christians and come to events run by them or be involved in projects run by a church, but are not looking to convert. So if conversion is our main measure of success, we are likely to feel like failures much of the time.

Becoming servants

So how do we develop a servant relationship with others? Let's be honest: we are unlikely to go around explaining to everyone that we are their servants, at their beck and call. They would almost certainly think we had gone mad and we would collapse from exhaustion after a few weeks if we tried to serve everyone. The main thing is that we choose to adopt the attitude and nature of servants. This links back to the idea of a spiritual scale. We are not at one end with everything to give and nothing to gain from others. We are on a par with others, at times helping, at other times being helped, just as a servant benefits from those they serve.

Going back to the prayer of Solomon, serving also means being in tune with God's will for others. That passage raises the thorny question of what happens when people of different faiths pray. Are they praying to the same God? More importantly, what does God make of their prayers? If God is omnipresent and omniscient, surely he hears what people are praying. Whether people of different faiths worship the same God is a topic of debate that I don't want to open up here. What I am interested in is what the God of the Bible does when people call out in prayer regardless of who, or what, they might be praying to. If Hindu parents in their temple make offerings to Ram and cry out for him to heal their child, does God take any notice of this? Does he ignore their cry or try not to listen? And if he does hear, what does he do?

Solomon framed this question in terms of people hearing about God and turning to the temple; he clearly expected people to hear about God's great deeds and know he was a deity worth praying to. Over the past few years I've met increasing numbers of vicars who relate how people of different faiths often come into church to pray. Sometimes they talk to people there, and when they do usually there is no talk of conversion but of being in a house of prayer. We could conclude from 1 Kings that these are prayers that will be answered, but what about those prayed not in the context of church or in connection with the Christian faith? Is it possible to consider that God may choose to answer those prayers as well? Part of being a servant is being in tune with what God is doing and serving others as a response to his prompting. When Jesus calls us to serve, this isn't a neutral act but a deeply spiritual calling – it's about joining with him in his serving and being obedient to his prompting to serve others. Maybe there are times when God hears the prayers of others and his answer to them is to call us to serve them.

It was a cold Sunday morning in December, and the churches in our area were holding a 'walking nativity'. People from the different churches dressed up as different characters from the nativity story and walked from their churches to the park where we met for a service. Joseph, Mary and a surprisingly compliant donkey went from our church, and a group of us walked alongside handing out vegetarian mince pies and chocolates to passers-by, the majority of whom were Muslims. I was with an Urdu-speaking friend when a woman in full hijab and her teenage son met us, and we offered them the mince pies. My friend explained to her in Urdu what they were; there was then a great flurry of chatter and the mum took a couple of mince pies for her son. After they had gone I asked what had happened. It turned out that the son had diabetes, and they'd been out shopping but had forgotten any sugar snacks for him and his sugar levels were getting low. The mum was getting anxious as they were a long way from home and they had no money for snacks, so she had been praying to Allah asking him for sugar for her son. Within minutes of praying we turned up and offered free sugary snacks for him! As far as she was concerned her prayers had been answered. Had they been? Were we God's answer to her prayer? We were able to serve her, not by declaring that we were her servants, but by being open to God's prompting and being willing to walk up the road with mince pies on a cold December morning. Being willing to serve is often costly and nearly always surprising.

Bringing it all together

Another useful passage we can turn to is Luke 17:11–19, where Jesus heals ten men who have leprosy. When I was a child in Sunday school this story came up fairly regularly, always as lessons in the importance of saying thank you. As a parent I'm very keen on teaching children to say thank you, but I don't think that that is what this passage is about. I do think it gives us a great example of Jesus' doing all the things we've mentioned in this chapter so far.

First, he took his disciples to Jerusalem by travelling along the border between Samaria and Galilee; this means they would have been likely to meet Samaritans. Samaritans were foreigners and enemies who worshipped God differently, but sort of the same. They were the people of a different faith who were to be avoided. But when the disciples followed Jesus, they found that it meant following him to places where they were likely to meet Samaritans. Jesus didn't avoid them; in fact, he deliberately sought them out. The disciples were no doubt nervous enough about meeting Samaritans and then the people who did come out to meet them had the dreaded disease of leprosy. Could the day have got any worse for them?

What did Jesus do when the men cried out? He did what they asked and, moreover, he had pity – not just a sympathetic pity but a love and concern that turns pity to action. He told them to go to show themselves to the priests; they were the ones who could declare someone free from disease. He was calling out to them that they were clean. He had served them and met their needs. Then, famously, only one returned to say thanks, and in the way Luke writes it this is a scandal. 'He threw himself at Jesus' feet and thanked him – and he was a Samaritan' (Luke 17:16). So now we have seen something else about Jesus: he made no distinction between the Jewish and Samaritan men; he healed all unconditionally. There was no suggestion that this man should have to consider who Jesus was first, or repent of his ways. Jesus' healing was for all. This unconditional attitude continued even after it's revealed that he was a Samaritan and has been healed.

The encounter concludes with one of the most surprising things Jesus says. Picture the scene. Jesus is standing there with a man kneeling in front of him, a Samaritan who has just experienced healing and is thanking Jesus. Surely the most natural thing would have been for Jesus to say, 'Come, follow me.' Here was someone who was an evangelist's dream! So what does Jesus say? 'Rise and go; your faith has made you well.' Go. Back to Samaria. Away from Jesus. What was he thinking of? I suspect what he was thinking of was the man in front of him, a man who had been forced to live away from his friends and family because of leprosy and was now free to go home. What Jesus does is to love this man and give him what he wants – full healing, which includes healing the relationships with people he's been forced to live apart from.

I'm sure if I'd been there I'd have run after the man and explained who it was that had healed him. I'd have probably produced a tract to share with him and got him to say a prayer of commitment and sign up to a discipleship course. I'd want to get him in; Jesus wanted to love him and serve him unconditionally. But in doing this Jesus didn't hide who he was; he didn't pretend to be a secular physician. The man knew that he had been healed miraculously by Jesus. Jesus was able to love and serve and be faithful to who he was, to love his heavenly Father and love his Samaritan neighbour.

If we only ask the question at the start of this chapter, namely who gets to heaven, then this encounter is bizarre or we perhaps conclude that Jesus failed in his evangelism. Will we meet the Samaritan man in heaven? We don't know, because the passage doesn't tackle that question. What it does deal with is how we treat outcasts, people in need, people different from us, and how we do that without denying our faith or hiding our trust in Jesus. It shows us that to be a Christian in a multifaith society is nothing new, but it's exactly the kind of place Jesus takes his disciples to and where amazing things happen that draw us closer to our neighbours and to God. It shows us that wondering whether someone's in heaven might be God's problem and not ours, which is why we rarely get told who's been saved.

But for all its richness this also isn't the only thing Jesus said or did. Before he returned to heaven, Jesus gave his disciples the great commission, to 'go and make disciples of all nations, baptising them in the name of the Father and of the Son and of the Holy Spirit' (Matthew 28:19). For some people this is where our encounters become more exciting, for others it is far more controversial. Chapter 4 will look at how we can undertake evangelism among people of different faiths, but before we think about how we do it, we need to return to the question posed at the start of Chapter 1 – Who's going to heaven? If we're 'in', are they by implication 'out'?

Questions

- What would it mean for you to love your neighbours of other faiths unconditionally? What would this love look like?

- Which would you prefer your ministry to be like, that of a doctor or that of a servant? If you were to ask people you know how you could serve them, what might they say?

- What do you think God does with the prayers of non-Christians? Could you ever be an answer to those prayers?

3

Them and us?

The young teacher turned up at the synagogue in the village where he had grown up. People were looking forward to hearing him, as news had spread of how good he was at preaching and the people were keen to hear the 'local boy made good'. At the usual point in the service he was given the scroll and started to read. The way he read impressed everyone; clearly the stories about him were true; a great teacher had come from their village. But the mood of pride didn't last. As he began to teach about the passage he had read, the congregation got more and more agitated. People whispered angrily and then voices were raised. Eventually they rushed up and seized this young upstart preacher and dragged him to the edge of the village. A small cliff was there, high enough that you wouldn't survive the fall. Throwing him from there would stop his appalling words once and for all. But as they got near the edge they seemed to lose their grip of his clothes. Try as they might they couldn't hold him, although he didn't seem to be struggling. The next thing anyone knew he was walking away from the cliff, away from the village and away from them.

This is what happens to Jesus in Luke 4:14–30 when he reads from Isaiah the passage that proclaims the year of the Lord's favour – when prisoners are set free, the blind recover their sight, good news is proclaimed to the poor and the oppressed are freed. So how is it that within just a few short words the people are trying to throw him off a cliff? What could be so offensive that they would turn so violently against him? Quite simply, he explained that in God's eyes the world is not about 'them and us'. He reminded the congregation that time and again the words of Isaiah had come true, not for the people of Israel but for foreigners – for Naaman, healed of leprosy, and for the widow of Zarephath, sustained during a famine. God's blessing, healing and provision wasn't just for 'us' but for all people, sometimes to the exclusion of his people.

Many years ago I was a young leader on a Christian camp, where a well-known evangelical preacher came to train us in evangelism. He started by saying that evangelism was really simple. He drew a line down the middle of a flip chart and drew some dots on either side. 'On this side,' he explained pointing to one side of the line, 'are Christians. On the other are non-Christians. Our task is to get people to cross the line; that's it.' It did seem straightforward when put like that, but even then I had a nagging sensation that life might not be quite as straightforward as a line on a flip chart.

The people in that synagogue wanted to cling to a message that the world was divided into two – *them* on the other side of the line and outside God's provision and care; and *us* on this side of the line, God's people blessed by him – and no one crossed the line. To suggest otherwise was so offensive that the preacher, Jesus, had to be got rid of, even thrown off a cliff. (Please note this is only a comment on the people in that synagogue, and not on wider Jewish attitudes towards this message which, no doubt, would have been varied and nuanced.)

In the Bible a tension is held between God's love and blessings for all (Genesis 12:3), and the particular way this promise is fulfilled through the people of Israel and then through Jesus. There is both breadth and narrowness to God's activity and somehow we have to find ways to comprehend and accept both. As Clark Pinnock states, 'The overall point is that according to the Old Testament God is in dialogue with all the peoples of the earth. What he is doing in the call of Abram and the election of Israel is not in opposition to the salvation of the world but on behalf of it.'[4] This is what I think Jesus was trying to open people's eyes to in Nazareth, that while we may be part of God's people (now manifested in the church) that doesn't mean we're the only ones God loves or cares for. The problem with focusing on who is going to heaven is that it forces us to see the world in terms of who is 'in' and who is 'out'. In the context of living among people of different faiths it can push us into attitudes a bit like those Jesus experienced, where we assume that we are the only ones God can, or would, bless. It pushes us back to seeing the world as a spiritual scale with 'them' at one end and 'us' at the other. It encourages us to be fixated on getting people across a line when the reality, as we shall see, is that life is often more complex than that for many people.

Learning from others

Over the years I've introduced many Christians to people of different faiths and taken them to visit different places of worship. A common experience is seeing them move from the assumption that the world is divided into neat camps, where we are on one side and they are on the other, to discovering that it's much more blurred. As we meet and talk we often discover that we share many values, ideas and even beliefs with people of different faiths. We find that their hopes, dreams and fears are often similar to ours. More than that, we often find that there are elements within their own faith that can inspire or even teach us. People talk about the inspiration to pray more having been to a mosque or to be more generous having been to a gurdwara. These visits are often a catalyst for changing people's world views. Being willing to step into a new place and to meet someone from another faith can enable us to recognise the faults in the way we have been viewing the world (to stop using a 'spiritual scale') and to start to look for the good and inspiring in others.

Learning from people from another faith, or even being inspired by them, is not new; there are plenty of biblical precedents. Gerald McDermott highlights how in the Old Testament there are a number of people outside the Jewish tradition who are seen as an inspiration and example for God's people, including Noah, Job,

Ruth and Naaman.[5] He goes on to highlight some examples from the New Testament, including the centurion seeking healing for his servant in Luke 7:1–10. There is no indication that the centurion saw Jesus as anything other than a miracle worker and he was one of the many who went to Jesus for help without the text's explicitly acknowledging that they became one of his followers. Yet Jesus praises the faith of the centurion, stating that he had not seen such faith in Israel, clearly indicating that the centurion was an 'outsider', presumably worshipping the Roman gods. Jesus doesn't demand that the centurion renounce his beliefs or convert, but sees something positive in his expression of faith in Jesus' power to heal, and Jesus applauds him, publicly, for it.

When in Athens, Paul speaks to the people about their altar to an unknown god. While talking to them, he quotes their own poets to back up his argument (Acts 17:22–31). He was clearly willing to read their texts and find things useful in them. Although he was inviting people to convert, Paul's starting point was to acknowledge that they had something within their own beliefs that was positive, even if unknown and uncertain. Rather than dismiss their poets, he reads them, quotes them and even affirms them as speaking words of truth that can lead people to God.

Perhaps one of the most intriguing examples of the outsider being held up as an example is the parable of the good Samaritan (Luke 10:25–37). This well-known parable is usually used to teach that our neighbours include all those we come across, even those we think of as enemies, and that we should show love to all of them. Clearly, that is a key message of this parable, but what I find intriguing is the characters Jesus chose, particularly the Samaritan. If the message was just to love your neighbour whoever they are, then it would have made much more sense to the listeners if the victim had been a Samaritan who was cared for by either a priest or a Levite. That version of the story would have taught us to love our neighbours of different faiths and cultures, but also it would have reinforced a message that it is God's people who do God's work, so we should copy their example. But Jesus subverts that idea. In his account it's the outsider, the foreigner who doesn't worship God properly, who lives the way God wants. In the midst of teaching about what it means to love a neighbour, Jesus also reinforces his teaching that life is not about simple categories of 'them' and 'us'. Sometimes 'they' get it right and 'we' get it wrong; there is no spiritual scale with us at one end and them at the other. We can all exhibit behaviour of which God approves or disapproves.

In fact, there's something even more subversive going on here. The encounter with the expert in the law doesn't start with a discussion about neighbourliness. It actually begins with the question, 'What must I do to inherit eternal life?' (Luke 10:25) Whatever follows, that question is uppermost in the man's mind; that is what he wants to find out about. Given that, wouldn't it have made even more sense to make sure the characters that behave according to God's law (and therefore inherit eternal life) were Jewish? What on earth could Jesus be suggesting? Is it possible that someone from another faith could be living so close to God's way that they inherit eternal life?

We see this possibility also suggested in the parable of the sheep and the goats (Matthew 25:31–46). The parable opens with all the nations of the world gathered before the Son of Man on his throne. There is no comment here on what people believe, but rather on their behaviour and practice. In fact, when Jesus calls to the 'sheep', telling them that they are blessed by God and can go to eternal life, they express surprise and aren't sure why they've been called. The implication here is that there will be those Jesus calls whose life has been lived in accordance with his will even though they might not have acknowledged him as king and saviour during their lifetime.

It's dangerous to develop an entire theology from one or two parables or verses, so I don't want to do that here. But I want to suggest that, however much we want to draw lines on flip charts or try to decide who's 'in' or 'out' of God's kingdom, the Bible has a habit of mixing things up. God is seen treating people as people, not theological categories; his compassion for all people is shown to have no bounds, and the people he created in his image but who do not know him still bear something of that image that can be seen and learned from. A spiritual scale that presents other faiths as spiritually bad is at odds with the way these parables portray and speak of them. Jesus isn't saying that they are perfect, but their example is something being held up for us to see as positive and to learn from. They cannot be considered as spiritually neutral and certainly not as entirely spiritually bad.

What about us?

Is it possible for us today to learn from or be inspired by our encounters with people of different faiths? A few years ago, I interviewed a number of Christian teenagers about their friendships with Muslims. One thing that stood out was that those who were the most convinced that only Christians go to heaven – and that everyone else, including Muslims, will be in hell – were also those who saw positive things in the faith of their Muslim friends. They could even articulate how their own faith had been deepened and enriched by the faith of their Muslim friends. I've often caricatured their attitude as 'You might be going to hell, but you've got something good to teach me on the way.' It would be easy to assume that these teenagers lived with a spiritual scale that bracketed out other faiths as bad, yet they were able to be far more nuanced than that. They could discern the good within their friends that could inspire and teach them.

In his book, *A Heart Broken Open*, Ray Gaston describes his trip to Iraq during the second Gulf war, having been invited to go on a pilgrimage to Karbala, an important Shia pilgrimage site. Ray describes the Christian faith as 'a spirituality that struggles with the realities of our world – its hatred, violence and confusion – and offers a way of redeeming this through meeting God in our active identification with the marginalised and in our refusal to use violence'.[6] He goes on to describe meetings with people who have faced unimaginable suffering, yet it was in the Muslim shrine of Lady Zaynab listening to Muslims singing devotional songs with a deep sense of lament that Ray describes how his heart was broken open by God for the people of Iraq. For Ray it was clearly God touching his heart, but it could only happen in such a way by his being present in that place with those people.

In 2014 I had the privilege of being taken on an interfaith pilgrimage to the Sikh Golden Temple at Amritsar in northern India. The pilgrimage was led by Bhai Sahib Mohinder Singh and other members of the Guru Nanak Nishkam Sewak Jatha (GNNSJ) gurdwara in Birmingham. Visiting Amritsar is amazing; the first glimpse of the Golden Temple really does take your breath away. We were treated to a full VIP tour of the temple, and as we were there for Diwali we experienced the celebrations that go on way into the night.

Yet for me the most moving moment was when a couple of Sikh friends and I decided to go for a walk in the courtyard of the temple at about 11.30 pm. It was still warm and fairly busy, but much quieter and calmer than in the middle of the day. One of my friends suggested that we should try to go into the actual Golden Temple as during the night, every night, volunteers clean it and apparently this was worth seeing. So off we went, and once again entering the Golden Temple left me slightly breathless because of its beauty. But what I hadn't expected was the intensity of the activity going on inside. Performing acts of service, or *seva*, is a fundamental part of Sikhism and every night volunteers go to the temple and clean every inch of it as an act of *seva*. Dozens of people were removing drapes, polishing the gold and the crystal lampshades. As they worked, with almost no speaking, a group sat in the middle of the temple and sang hymns from the Sikh scriptures, the Guru Granth Sahib.

We sat for about half an hour listening to the singing and watching the cleaners – an incredibly moving and uplifting experience. There was something about the passion of the singing, the willingness to work into the night and the combination of worship and service that was inspiring. It made me reflect on my attitude to serving and how rarely I link it so closely to worship. I also thought of my attitude to sacred spaces, which I can be quite casual about, yet there I felt as if I was in the presence of people preparing the throne room of a king, performing a sacred act in a sacred place. Two years on I still recall that moment and those emotions with great clarity; I'm still inspired by what I saw and continue to be challenged about what it would mean for me to worship and serve in that way and whether my evangelical Christianity has lost something of the awe and majesty of God that I experienced in the Golden Temple.

I've also spoken to many Christians over the years who have been inspired or challenged by the example or teachings of different faiths, whether the Muslim discipline of fasting during Ramadan and praying five times a day, the generosity of *langar* (free kitchens) and *seva* in Sikhism or the way Hindus set aside space at home for prayer and worship. These and other examples from other religions have led many Christians to be thankful for their friends of other faiths who have helped them deepen their own Christian faith. This kind of approach, where we look for the good in others, can happen only when we reject the idea of a spiritual scale and acknowledge that we don't have all the answers and that others have much that we can benefit from.

So who is going to heaven?

The other questions I've tackled will often have a far greater impact on the way we live than this one. However, I've said I'll answer it, so here goes. The first part of the answer, and I might be accused of avoiding it again, is that it's not really my place to say; this is in God's hands. Fortunately for everyone, I don't get any say in who gets into heaven (and neither does anyone else). We can have every idea and theology we like but in the end it's all down to God.

However, the Bible does teach that there is the guarantee of salvation, getting to heaven, for those who are believers in, and followers of, Jesus (John 3:16; Romans 10:9–10). There is clearly the expectation that believing and calling on the name of the Lord in themselves aren't sufficient for salvation, but have to lead to active following or discipleship (James 2:19, 26; Matthew 7:21).

So I often say to friends of different faiths that the Bible guarantees salvation to those who follow Jesus, but that isn't the same as saying everyone who doesn't is going to hell. If that were the case, surely Jesus would have begged the Roman centurion or the Samaritans he met to convert or he would have pursued the rich young ruler until he changed his mind. Also one of the few people we know is definitely going to be there is the thief on the cross, whose entire belief, commitment and confession was 'Jesus, remember me when you come into your kingdom' (Luke 23:42). In the kingdom parables in Matthew there are specific references to God separating the righteous from the wicked with the wicked being punished (Matthew 13:36–52), but I would be very cautious about labelling entire groups of people as wicked or evil. Certainly, the implication from both parables is that the righteous and wicked are largely inseparable; it is only at the end that God can judge and that is definitely not our job, as is clearly stated in Matthew 7:1–2. Further on in Matthew 7, Jesus teaches that there will be good and bad disciples and true and false prophets. In other words, it's going to be confusing to work out who's saved. The chapter ends with the parable of the house on the rock, where judgement is for those who hear God's word and don't put it into practice, not for those who haven't heard.

I could go on in this vein, but I hope I've begun to show that there is the guarantee of salvation for those who believe and follow Jesus, and there is punishment for the wicked, but there is the tantalising possibility of salvation for others who haven't heard or who are following Jesus' example without explicitly being a disciple of Jesus (like the obedient son in Matthew 21:28-31). I firmly believe that whoever is in heaven and whatever they believed before they got there, they will be there because Jesus says to the Father, 'They're with me; my blood was shed for all.'

Does this mean that there is no need for us to share our faith with others, if there's the chance they'll get to heaven anyway? Only if we think that being a Christian is nothing more than getting an entry ticket to an eternal life that starts when we die. Jesus, and the rest of the Bible, don't just talk about life after death but have a huge amount to say about how we live now. Choosing to follow Jesus, and therefore being filled with the Holy Spirit, transforms life now in ways that are beneficial for everyone. Even if I think they might get to heaven, I'd love for people to know the love of Jesus now, so I'll carry on sharing my faith with them.

I recognise that not everyone will agree with my views, and I know that my views change and develop the more I study scripture and follow Jesus. But, when asked what was the greatest command, Jesus didn't say, 'Have a correct theology of salvation' but 'Love God and love your neighbour.'

Questions:

- How do you react when you hear preachers say things that go against your preconceived ideas of what God is like?

- Whom have you met who isn't a Christian but has inspired you by their words or actions?

- Arrange to visit a place of worship of another faith, but go with an enquiring attitude. What will you learn and how will your own faith grow through the visit?

4

The great commission

The official rode in his chariot reading the scroll he'd recently received. He knew it was part of the sacred Jewish scriptures and he found the poetry beguiling, but he couldn't work out the meaning. It talked about a lamb that was silent as it was slaughtered and of a man deprived of justice. He had no idea what it all meant. As he was pondering this the official heard footsteps and heavy breathing. To his utter surprise a man was beside his chariot, running faster than anyone he'd ever seen. Before the official could speak, the runner asked him if he understood what he was reading. The question seemed a bit impertinent, but the official shrugged and said he had no one to explain it to him. He asked the runner to jump into the chariot and sit beside him. The day then took another surprising turn, as this unknown runner explained how the text referred to the one called Jesus that the official had heard about. Again amazed, the official decided that he too wanted to be a follower of Jesus, and he insisted that this strange running man baptise him in the nearest river. The chariot stopped and down they both went into the stream, where the official was baptised and went home rejoicing at what had happened.

What this chapter is and isn't about

In this chapter, I want to try to recognise both the calling Christians have to obey the great commission and the controversy and difficulties that this can cause. For some, like Philip, the running man in the above story (adapted from Acts 8:26–40), it's a calling and a joy to share the good news of Jesus with people from all backgrounds and lead them to faith in Christ. For others, it's seen as an arrogant act where we ignore the beliefs of others and impose our own ideas on people. It's easy to dismiss either side of the argument, to demand that evangelism stop or to run roughshod over the concerns and anxieties of those opposed to evangelism. However, I don't think that either of those positions is viable or ethical. I don't believe that as evangelists we can just ignore the hurt and anger people feel; we have to love our neighbour even when they oppose what we do. But neither can we ignore people's deep sense of calling to evangelism. If we believe that people should be free to practise their faith we can't then arbitrarily decree which bits they can or can't do, providing they operate within the law.

I'm conscious that that last sentence raises as many questions as it tries to answer, given the different laws and changing attitudes in society, so let me set the context for this chapter. I'm writing this in Britain, primarily for Christians living and working here. If you're reading this elsewhere in the world it's lovely that you are but you will need to reflect on what the great commission might look like in your context. There are countries where evangelism is illegal and where people face serious punishment for breaking the law. Having never lived or worked in those countries, I'm not prepared to tell Christians who do how they should obey the great commission; rather, I would want to sit and learn from them about how they work this out.

Finally, before we really get going, I'm aware that this topic is controversial among Christians. I have many friends who have a strong calling to evangelism and for whom it is not an optional extra, like some theological rucksack they can take off when asked. I also have Christian friends who think that evangelism among people of different faiths is unethical and theologically problematic, as they feel it is their calling to affirm the genuine faith that other people have and that loving their neighbour is the highest calling for them. I'm more at the evangelist end of the spectrum (although I'm not sure I'm very good at it). I'm very happy to share with people the good news of Jesus and to offer them the chance to follow Jesus if they want to, but I have lots of questions and concerns about the way evangelism is done and the attitudes and language used by some people as they seek to obey the great commission. I was once asked by a missionary who had moved to Birmingham if I could help him target Mirpuri Muslims for evangelism. I said I could help him make friends, but could never help anyone target anybody. Sadly, that kind of language with aggressive undertones, which treats people as objects, targets even, is all too common among some groups of evangelists, and causes me much concern. In this chapter, I'm primarily speaking to Christians in Britain who have a sense that they probably ought to do something about the great commission but have questions, doubts or concerns about how to go about it. So let's crack on.

How would you feel?

Before we think about how we share our faith I want to turn the tables briefly. Just spend a few minutes picturing the congregation of the church you attend – the leaders, musicians, children, adults and so on. Get a really clear picture, perhaps of you all together on a Sunday. Now imagine what would happen if one Sunday it was announced that six members of your church, including a leader, had all converted to another faith. How do you think people would react? What questions would that raise? How would people feel about what the leader had done? How would people feel when they saw those people out promoting their new faith in the street? How would their families feel?

I've presented this idea on many occasions and the overwhelming response to the questions I raise is negative. People talk about feeling confused, betrayed, doubting their own faith, concerned as to what the people have converted to and so on. When we consider the implications of conversion, we need to recognise the emotional and spiritual upset an event such as this would cause us. We can then begin to understand some of the reasons why people of other faiths are also wary of evangelism. The kinds of emotions described above would potentially also be found in a temple, mosque, gurdwara or other place of worship if six people converted to Christianity. Conversion is about people, so there is bound to be an emotional response to conversion, positive for the person converting but often painful for the friends and family of the convert. I said in the Introduction that Jesus' command to 'do to others as you would have them do to you' (Luke 6:31) is challenging and important, and never more so, I believe, than when we are talking about evangelism.

Think back to the scenario in your church. What would you have wanted the people of another faith who were out sharing that faith to do? Would you have wanted them to come and talk to the whole church? Or talk to the families of those thinking of converting? Or perhaps you'd rather they left you alone? When we ask these questions we start to grapple with Jesus' question: what would it mean to do to others as you would have them do to you? It at least means that any evangelism we do to others we have to be happy for them to do to us. If you want to think about the way you do evangelism, go and be evangelised and reflect on what the process was like. Whether it's being preached at in the street, handed a tract or visited at home, seriously consider how you feel when people do these things to you or your friends and family; then apply Jesus' teaching, 'Do to others as you would have them do to you.'

There are lots of ways of doing evangelism (or sharing your faith, depending on your preferred terminology) and some are more effective or endearing than others. Have you ever stopped to consider what effect your style of evangelism has on other people – not just the spiritual effect of whether they choose to convert, but whether they actually appreciate what you're doing? This doesn't just mean that they might think you're being too assertive; several of my Muslim friends often ask why Christians are hesitant about their faith and would be happy for us to be more open and confident about telling people what we believe. However, they don't want to be criticised for their beliefs, nor treated in a patronising or arrogant way. They can appreciate ways in which we do evangelism even if they question or reject the message.

Objections to evangelism

Having got us to think about how we might feel if someone converted *from* Christianity, I want to outline some other reasons why people might object to evangelism or conversion. I mention both, as some people are happy with the idea of Christians doing evangelism as long as it's other people who convert; others object to the idea of evangelism itself even if it's done in the friendliest way. In 2007 the Hindu Council UK produced a discussion paper for leaders from different faiths in which there is a section challenging the concept of evangelism, particularly when undertaken by Christians or Muslims. The paper goes as far as to say, 'I believe that to seek to convert already God-loving people to another faith is a sin, an evil act done simply to advance one's own club.'[7] Not all Hindus would agree with this position, but it's a view held by some people of different faiths: that the very act of evangelism is deeply problematic, if not sinful.

Betrayal

For many people the idea that someone would leave the faith of their family and community and choose another one carries with it a tremendous sense of betrayal, as if the beliefs, practices and religious life of the family are inadequate and those of another religion and culture are better.

It's worth remembering that for many people their religious life is not just a set of theological beliefs but a whole world of behaviours and practices that includes attending places of worship, family occasions, celebrations and so on. There's a danger that we think of conversion as nothing more than a personal choice that affects just our spiritual life. For someone converting from another faith, however, it means no longer going with the family to the gurdwara or not taking part with family celebrations for Eid.

A man who had converted from Hinduism to Christianity told me about the day he chose to tell his parents. He drove back to their house, but in their tradition you honour the Hindu deity by the front door before you enter the house. This was something he no longer wanted to do, and when his parents asked why he hadn't done it he ended up telling them, on the doormat before even entering the house, that he had become a Christian. That is not the best place to have that discussion, but it shows that conversion is not just a cerebral or internal spiritual matter but affects the behaviour of the convert in ways that the family and community can find bewildering or hurtful.

In a group discussion between Sikhs, Muslims and Christians about conversion, one of the Sikhs said he wouldn't object if a family member converted; for him, we all worship the one god so it didn't matter whether you were Sikh, Muslim or Christian. What if, asked another member of the group, that person no longer wanted to go to the gurdwara or didn't want to bow down when they entered it for a wedding? At that point, the Sikh participant admitted he'd find it hard. He suddenly realised that conversion affects behaviour, and that can be painful.

I've learnt over recent months that for many families, particularly the Muslims I listen to, the issue is not necessarily joining Christianity but leaving Islam. There are a number of online forums for ex-Muslims who have left Islam and become secular, who face similar challenges from families to those experienced by converts to Christianity. The objection might not be that a family member has become a Christian but that they have left the faith of their family.

Salvation

When we talk about conversion we are back to discussions about who's going to be in heaven. If you come from a tradition that says that it is only through following your religion that you get to heaven, then watching a family member leave that religion is going to be painful. We all want heaven to be full of the people we love; the idea of spending eternity away from a child is, for many people, unimaginably painful. So it's understandable that people will be upset that a family member is choosing to leave that path. It's the same reason why many Christian parents feel so sad when their children turn away from Jesus and reject their faith. We want them to be with us in heaven; the idea of not being with them is almost unbearable.

Culture

Part of the issue for many people is culture as much as theology or spirituality. Christianity has its own cultures, often Western, that at best can be puzzling (even for those of us born and brought up in them) or at worst clash with the culture of the family. Whether that's a family from Asia, Africa or the Middle East, the chances are that there will be a variety of cultural norms that are very different from those of British Christianity. Coupled with that is the fact that to those outside, much of Christianity in Britain is indistinguishable from mainstream British society. As Christians we might object to this, but many people still consider Britain to be a Christian country and see British culture as a reflection of Christianity. How we respond to this cultural divide is something we'll look at in Chapter 7.

Apostasy

The issue of apostasy within Islam has been argued over by Muslims and non-Muslims alike. Tim Green provides an excellent summary of the debate, in which he explains that an apostate was considered as one who had left Islam, which also meant rejecting the political

Islamic rulers. At a time of war and political turmoil, this was treason. 'Loyalty to Allah meant loyalty to his ruler on earth. Rejection of the one necessarily implied rejection of the other, so apostasy spelt treason.'[8] He goes on to explain that there has been debate within Islam as to whether the punishment should be carried out in this life or in the next by Allah, and in contemporary societies whether apostasy is only for treason or for those who choose to leave Islam.

Tim outlines how attitudes are changing, with some Muslim leaders affirming the right of people to convert without harassment. I've noticed this shift in attitudes here in Birmingham, which is partly the result of more assertive *Da'wah* activity by Muslims and partly because of social media. As Muslims are becoming more confident in inviting people to convert from other faiths to Islam, they realise the hypocrisy of encouraging conversion in one direction but opposing it in the other. At the same time, stories of people converting from one religion to another are increasingly shared on social media, normalising the experience as well as highlighting the plight of converts.

The way converts from Islam to Christianity are treated in the UK and in other parts of the world is a cause of pain and embarrassment for some Muslims, who are increasingly willing to speak out on social media about this issue. Many people are still opposed to conversion for lots of different reasons, but there is a noticeable shift in attitudes from a few years ago.

A Muslim friend told me of a conversation he had with someone we both knew who was a convert to Christianity; this person told him how anxious he was of mixing with Muslims for fear of reprisals for being a convert. My Muslim friend was deeply upset that the assumption was that he and others would reject this person because they were a convert, when he was more than willing to get to know him and would not wish to cause him any harm.

Cultural and religious genocide

Perhaps one of the more controversial, but nevertheless important, critiques of evangelism is that if it were successful it would lead to a cultural and religious genocide. This argument tends to come from certain Jewish and Sikh groups, faiths that are relatively small in number from a global perspective and have clear links between religion and ethnicity. The argument goes that if the great commission was totally successful and everyone converted to Christianity then there would be no more Sikhism or Judaism. The traditions, beliefs and cultures of these people would vanish, as would their distinctive ethnic tie to their religion. Not all Sikhs or Jews would use this language, but it is a critique that we need to be aware of.

Ethical evangelism?

Having laid out several reasons why people object to evangelism and conversion I now want to look at how we might be faithful to the great commission and undertake evangelism while also obeying the commands to love God and our neighbour. Is it possible to do evangelism in a way that demonstrates a love for our neighbour?

As an aside, while sharing our faith can be an act of love, I question whether it always feels like that. For an act of love to be genuine, the recipient has to be able to see it as that. A small gift from someone you love means more than a big gift from a stranger. The act has to have a context of love for it to be loving. In other words, doing evangelism in a way that annoys or upsets people is not a loving gesture, even if you think you are offering them an amazing gift. It's just an irritating offer from someone who doesn't seem to care. As a Hindu friend of mine once said, 'Why would I invite you to my house when you think I'm an idol worshipper, a sinner and need to convert?' A challenging question. And if we're honest, that is how many Christians would see him, but he knows that and he doesn't like it or want it. He certainly doesn't feel that many Christians love him as they love themselves.

I was once at a meal with some young adults of different faiths who were on a leadership course I was running. There were Christians, Muslims, Sikhs and a Buddhist in the group. During the meal the issue of conversion came up and a Sikh friend turned to me and said, 'I understand that if you saw someone who had no faith and was down on their luck, homeless and a drug addict, that you'd want them to become a Christian, but do you want me to convert?' My friend is a passionate Sikh who, like all Sikhs, does not do evangelism, so it was a great question which everyone else wanted to hear my answer to.

My answer was this: 'I think being a Christian is the best thing ever; I find it gives me hope and purpose and an assurance of salvation, so I'd love everyone to find that too. So, yes, I'd like that for you, but no more than for anyone else; you're not a target. But also it's optional. I'm not going to force you to convert; you're allowed to say no. And another thing: if you want me to shut up about my faith I will.'

My friend appreciated that answer and said she didn't want me to stop talking about my faith, but could now understand my views on evangelism. That explanation of my approach to evangelism was a quick attempt to summarise how I think one can share the good news of Jesus in a loving and ethical way.

In 2009 I was involved in producing the Christian Muslim Forum's guidelines for ethical witness. As a group, we recognised that Christians and Muslims were engaged in evangelism or *Da'wah* and we wanted to affirm people's right to do that. But we also recognised that there were good and bad ways of doing this. It could be done in an underhand, coercive or manipulative way, or it could be done with openness, honesty and integrity. The document we produced listed ten points for Christians and Muslims to consider as guidelines for how they could share their faith ethically:

1   We bear witness to, and proclaim our faith not only through words but through our attitudes, actions and lifestyles.

2   We cannot convert people, only God can do that. In our language and methods we should recognise that people's choice of faith is primarily a matter between themselves and God.

3   Sharing our faith should never be coercive; this is especially important when working with children, young people and vulnerable adults. Everyone should have the choice to accept or reject the message we proclaim and we will accept people's choices without resentment.

4   Whilst we might care for people in need or who are facing personal crises, we should never manipulate these situations in order to gain a convert.

5   Invitations to convert should never be linked with financial, material or other inducements; it is a decision of the heart and mind alone.

6   We will speak of our faith without demeaning or ridiculing the faiths of others.

7   We will speak clearly and honestly about our faith, even when that is uncomfortable or controversial.

8   We will be honest about our motivations for activities and we will inform people when events will include the sharing of faith.

9   Whilst recognising that either community will naturally rejoice with and support those who have chosen to join them, we will be sensitive to the loss that others may feel.

10 Whilst we may feel hurt when someone we know and love chooses to leave our faith, we will respect their decision and will not force them to stay or harass them afterwards.[9]

This document was important, as it was agreed by senior leaders of both faiths and has been endorsed and used by a number of other groups since. It sought to take seriously the call to evangelism while recognising the controversy it can cause.

Turning to scripture

Of course, behaving ethically while sharing the gospel is nothing new and we can look to the Bible for further inspiration. In 1 Thessalonians 2:1–12 Paul reminds the Christians in Thessalonica how he, Silas and Timothy had behaved when they had been with them. It's a challenging passage about how to behave when sharing the gospel. Paul makes it clear that they had pure motives, weren't trying to trick them and didn't use flattery or assert their authority over them. On the contrary, they loved the Thessalonians and cared for them, sharing both the gospel and their lives. Paul even goes so far as to state, 'You are witnesses, and so is God, of how holy, righteous and blameless we were among you who believed' (1 Thessalonians 2:10). Clearly Paul was taking seriously the idea that the way the gospel was shared was, perhaps, as important as the message itself. Certainly the two things couldn't be disentangled, so he was keen to make sure and to point out that the gospel had been shared in a way that was consistent with the imperative to love our neighbour.

This passage is a wonderful checklist that we can use to evaluate the way we share our faith. Can we say with all honesty that we have pure motives, that we don't use flattery or trickery and that we are holy and blameless in the way we behave? Do we love and care for our Jewish, Sikh or Buddhist neighbours as a mother might, so much so that we want to share our lives as well as the gospel? This is all challenging stuff, but it gives us a clear summons not to hold back from sharing our faith but to think about the way we do it.

At the start of this chapter I quoted a discussion paper from the Hindu Council UK which described evangelism as a sin. Evangelism is not a sin, but it can be done in sinful ways, for example, by exploiting or manipulating people. In 1 Thessalonians, Paul is clearly trying to demonstrate that he shared the gospel in a way that could not be construed as sinful, but that honoured the message of the gospel and was consistent with it.

What do I say?

It never ceases to amaze me how nervous Christians feel about speaking of their faith to people of another faith. When I talk about my work in churches, people are often surprised by what I do and think I'm doing God's work in a really difficult context. My reply is that I think I'm working in a situation where talking about faith is, on the whole, easy. Indeed, I always feel a bit of a fraud and a bit puzzled as to why they think it's so tough. One concern is that people of other faiths, and usually that means Muslims, will be offended if we speak about the Christian faith. In my experience nothing could be further from the truth; the vast majority of people are not sitting around waiting to be offended by Christians talking about what they believe, but are quite happy to chat about faith. So don't be anxious; on the whole this is going to be okay.

The next thing people say is that they don't know enough about their faith or the faith of the other person. If you think that sharing faith is about proving points or winning arguments, then worrying that you don't know enough is probably appropriate. Certainly, that's what I thought sharing faith with Muslims was about when I started this work back in the 1990s. I thought that the best thing to do was to prove that Christianity was right and that the other faith was wrong, so I needed all the clever arguments that I could find. The trouble was I wasn't very good at remembering them, and the people I was in conversation (or having an argument) with had heard them all before and had their answers prepared. The same was true of their questions about Christianity: they rehearsed them, I learned the answers and we went round and round in circles getting more and more frustrated. I was once listening to a sermon by the former Archbishop of Canterbury Rowan Williams, who said, 'Jesus didn't die on the cross so that we could win arguments in pubs. He came that we might have life in all its fullness.' I was in danger of reducing the Christian faith to arguments that I would try to win.

Eventually I learned that most people aren't convinced by arguments, however sophisticated or clever those arguments are, but they are willing to talk with people who are genuinely interested in them and who have something positive and interesting to share. It's easy to want to disprove the ideas or beliefs of other people, especially if we have decided that we are right and that they are wrong and that they have nothing to teach us. In my experience, however, when we start by telling people that their beliefs are wrong, few say, 'Really? Oh, thank you.' Instead, they become defensive and work harder to prove their beliefs are correct.

It's amazing how easily people slip into criticising other beliefs when talking about their own. I hear it from people of all faiths, and it's unhelpful. I firmly believe that the gospel is good news, so it can be proclaimed as good news without our having to criticise other beliefs for being bad news. I've found that when I work hard to speak about my faith positively it's much more interesting to others and opens up far more conversations. Try listening out for this in sermons or evangelistic talks, and you'll be surprised just how many people show that the gospel is good not on its own terms but only in comparison to other views. We should avoid this habit and have the confidence that the gospel is fully good news; even if there was nothing to compare it to it would still be good news. It's not the least worst or the best there is for now; it is the good news. Having the confidence to speak about it positively and enthusiastically is vital for all Christians, but particularly when speaking to people of different faiths.

I sometimes describe this by drawing two wiggly lines on a page, each heading off in a different direction. We might think that we are on a path to heaven and that people of another faith are on their path. (Whether you think that goes to heaven or not will depend on your particular theology – see Chapter 1.) This kind of approach tries to convince people that they are on the wrong path, and that once they have realised that they will choose to leave that path and join ours. The problem of this approach, as I see it, is that people don't like being told they're wrong, and that even if we convince them they are on the wrong path it doesn't necessarily follow that they'll want to join ours. I'd much rather talk about, and show, the Christian path in such a positive light that people start to enquire what it's all about and have a desire to join it.

When we start to speak of what we believe positively, it takes away the burden of having to know lots about another faith. While it's useful to know some of the basics of what other people believe, it's by no means essential. As I said in the Introduction, the best technique is to smile and ask; in a friendly way find out what they believe by just asking. This has several advantages. First, you don't need any prior knowledge, just a willingness to ask and listen. Second, it shows that you are more interested in them than you are in yourself; too much evangelism is about us when it ought to be about the people we're talking to. Third, it means that you find out what the person you are talking to actually believes rather than what a book might have told you. In all faiths there is huge diversity and people have different levels of knowledge. Just because someone's a Sikh, this does not mean they are fully versed in Sikh theology and wisdom.

Some people have unusual ideas they have picked up along the way that won't appear in any resource but that they hold to be true, and we have to go with that. I was once running a trip for Christian and Muslim teenagers and was talking to a Muslim volunteer about catering, and I said that I'd get the halal meat for the weekend. He told me, quite firmly, that I couldn't do that because if a Christian bought it, it would no longer be halal. I had never heard that before and, despite having asked numerous Muslims, have never heard it since. However, I had to work with him on that weekend, which meant letting him buy the meat. I only learned that by talking to him, but because I did so I was able to understand him and show him that I was willing to act in a way that, I hope, he thought demonstrated a love for my Muslim neighbour.

Truth or experience?

Many years ago I tried to use clever arguments with Muslim friends, as I described above. One of the frustrations I had was that we constantly ran into the same problem – however we tried to describe the truth of our faiths, we actually didn't agree on what constituted truth. My Muslim friends would say that Islam is so beautiful in its simplicity. There is one God, Allah, who has revealed his will through Mohammed so that we have the Qur'an in one language, Arabic. It's so simple and beautiful that it must be true. 'Ah, yes,' I would reply, 'but we have one God in Trinity, which is a concept so mind-bogglingly complex, and a Bible that several people were inspired over centuries to write in a variety of languages, yet it's consistent and faithful. There's no way that we could have all this without God. Its complexity demonstrates its truthfulness.' We could have argued until we were blue in the face, but we wouldn't have got anywhere because we didn't agree with each other's definition of truth.

I'm still convinced that the Bible is true, but I began to realise that that may not be the best starting point. Instead, when I asked them to tell me why they loved being a Muslim, and then I told them why I loved being a Christian, we were able to change the conversation. We decided just to assume that we believed the Bible or the Qur'an to be true and let each other explain what we found fulfilling within it. Suddenly, we were able to talk about our faith in a totally new way. We talked about things we believed to be true but within the context of our experience of faith; they became alive. Truths were not abstract arguments that we used to score points, but life-enhancing concepts that made sense in the context of our own experiences.

Learning to share my faith in this way, and helping others do the same, has been a revelation for me and many other people. It isn't about denying the truth but about finding ways of connection that make sense to those we are speaking to, and takes from us the burden of thinking we need to have done a course on evangelism or other faiths before we start. Your story of what God has done is enough to share with someone else. One of the great things about being a Christian is that our testimony doesn't stop the day we become a Christian; that's just one step on the path. So even if you've been a Christian a short while and think that you don't know much, just share that. You'll soon have more to share and your story will keep on growing, along with your knowledge of the Christian faith. If someone asks you a question you don't know the answer to, just say, 'I don't know.' That's not failure, it's honesty. It's also a great prompt to go and find out, and that is one of the ways talking to people of different faiths can deepen our knowledge and strengthen our faith.

Discussing in this way also gives me a way of responding to those street preachers who have set questions but are rarely interested in my answers. They have usually been taught a set list of questions and the expected answers that Christians give to them. If I sense that they have little interest in me or my answers, I don't answer their question but rather ask them what it is in their faith that inspires them. I then say that I want a chance to tell them why I love being a Christian, and I also suggest that we each give our answers without criticising the beliefs or practices of the other. In this way, more fruitful discussions sometimes develop, but even if they don't, at least it enables me to get out of trying to answer a list of set questions when no one is really listening.

Making connections

Once we learn to speak about our faith positively and to share our experiences or testimony, it's an easy step to start to look for connections between our faiths that can prompt a conversation.

I might ask a Sikh friend if they are going to a gurdwara and what happens there. When they explain to me about the singing and the prayers, it's easy then to talk about what happens in church. If I ask a Muslim how they're getting on fasting during Ramadan and why they fast, it's really easy then to talk about fasting in Christianity, where there are similarities with Islamic practice but also differences.

Talking about differences, whether of belief or practice, becomes not a competition or criticism but a point of interest. I once had a conversation with a Muslim leader where we talked about forgiveness – an easy place to start as it's a concept shared between our faiths. As we talked it became apparent that we had some differences in our beliefs, but these made for a fascinating conversation. I learned about Islamic teachings on seeking forgiveness from others and it challenged me to think about that practice in my life; meanwhile I was able to share Christian teaching on forgiveness in the light of Jesus' life, death and resurrection. Making a connection was the starting point that allowed us to talk about similarities and differences, but because we had the attitude of sharing our faith positively we were able to share profound truths in the context of our own story and in a way that kept the conversation going rather than closing it down.

Questions

- How do you feel when you encounter evangelists from other faiths? How might this knowledge inform the way you do evangelism?

- How would the imperative 'Do to others as you would have them do to you' affect the way you do evangelism?

- Why do you love being a Christian?

- Can you describe following Jesus as 'good news' without criticising others?

5

Doing dialogue

'Follow me,' he had said and, feeling strangely compelled, they had left their fishing business and followed this new rabbi. They knew others who had followed rabbis and had seen them mix with religious leaders and become respectable members of society. But this rabbi was different. Not only was his preaching something different, compelling, challenging and often very funny, but they'd seen him perform miracles. Yes, actually heal people in front of their eyes. But it wasn't all healing and good sermons: since following him, they'd been nearly drowned in a storm and met demon-possessed men, and now they were sitting at a meal in the local tax-collector's house! Not only that, but all sorts of corrupt business people and others they'd always avoided had turned up. What sort of rabbi was this who took them to meet people they'd been taught to avoid? Other religious leaders were critical of their eating with these people, but the rabbi was adamant: these were exactly the kinds of people God cared for and with whom he should sit and eat.

Back in the mid 1990s, when I started this work, the world was very different to how it is today. Apart from the obvious differences in technology – such as limited Internet and email access, no smartphones or social media – the big global issues back then were the end of the Cold War and the first Gulf war. Another difference was how divided Christians were in their approach to engaging with people of different faiths. Put simply, you were either an evangelical, who was primarily concerned with evangelism, or a liberal, whose main area of interest was interfaith dialogue, and the two camps rarely met, at least in a friendly and constructive way.

Dialogue had a reputation among evangelicals as compromising on the fundamentals of what you believed. Some thought that mixing with people of other faiths was not to be done unless you were preaching to them. The Christians who did get involved were thought to have 'sold out', and stories abounded of interfaith meetings in churches where the name Jesus couldn't be mentioned for fear of offending others. The image often used to describe, and decry, dialogue was that of paths up a mountain: we're all on different paths but it's the same mountain. Dialogue can help you appreciate the paths others are on and perhaps give you inspiration and direction for your path, but there is no need to change path as they all, ultimately, end at the same place. As you can imagine, that kind of talk was like a red rag to a bull to evangelists convinced that Jesus is 'the way and the truth and the life' (John 14:6). On the other hand, evangelists were often perceived by the dialogue community to be arrogant, unwilling to see the good in others, uninterested in what could be learned from other faiths and concerned only about preaching the gospel with one aim in mind – conversion.

Neither of these caricatures was entirely accurate or fair, but nor were they a million miles from the truth. They were exaggerated and inflated but not without some kernel of truth. As you can imagine, for a young, enthusiastic evangelical the prospect of dialogue was not appealing. When I read passages like Matthew 9:9–11, where Jesus is accused of mixing with undesirables, I saw only the part about Jesus calling the sinners; I didn't notice how significant it was that he was willing to sit and eat with people the other religious leaders were wary of. I'm not suggesting that all people of other faiths are bad people, but that there were (and still are) Christian leaders who think that they are best avoided.

What is dialogue?

While writing my thesis on dialogue, I tried to enthuse my wife, Sarah, with my latest ideas and theories. She listened patiently and asked, 'But isn't dialogue just talking?' To which the answer is, of course, yes; but once the academics and theologians had got involved, it was made to look a lot more complicated. Over the years the word 'dialogue' has taken on many meanings. The Dialogue Society produced a book on different approaches to dialogue and list around ten different theories of dialogue, none of which involves just sitting and chatting.[10] Despite the theological and practical divides between evangelism and dialogue, there have been attempts to build bridges and offer creative ways for these things to be brought closer together. In 1981 the Church of England outlined four guidelines for dialogue that are still useful for unpacking what this might mean for Christians. Their four guidelines are:

- dialogue begins when people meet each other;
- dialogue depends on mutual understanding and trust;
- dialogue makes it possible to share in service to the community;
- dialogue becomes the medium of authentic witness.[11]

These categories resonate with a lot of people as they start at the basic human level of meeting. Dialogue is not about developing theories of how one religion relates to another; it is fundamentally about people meeting. However formal, theological or philosophical dialogue meetings become, genuine dialogue requires people to meet. This might sound obvious, especially if you are someone who lives or works among people of different faiths and for whom this is everyday life, but for those who don't have natural encounters and rely on dialogue events to meet people of different faiths it's easy to focus on the event or the theory rather than on the encounters with other people.

So what makes 'interfaith dialogue' different from two people of different faiths chatting in the street? The answer, I think, lies in the intent of the people: in what way are they entering into the conversation and what do they expect out of it? A meeting of friends becomes dialogue when there is a meeting of equals who seek to understand the other person and to be transformed through the encounter. As Christians, we would also want to say that in dialogue one wants to discern God's activity in the life of the other person and in the encounter. Dialogue, in this context, isn't a casual meeting with no agenda or a lecture with no interaction. It's an intentional meeting to discuss topics in order to share ideas and to engage with the beliefs of others.

Defined in this way, dialogue does not mean giving up everything we believe but does mean being willing to meet and listen to our neighbours. In some ways, it can be seen as a practical way to bring together the two greatest commands: to love the Lord your God and to love your neighbour as yourself.

Speaking truths

When I first went, nervously, to a Christian–Muslim dialogue event, I was on full alert for a moment when I would be asked to compromise things that I held most dear. To my great surprise not only did that not happen, but I had lots of opportunities to explain what I believed to Muslims who were genuinely interested. I also learned much from them and came away transformed by the encounter, still a Christian but with a profound sense of having been in a place where God was at work in and through our conversations. The act of engaging in dialogue with Muslims was not just interesting or useful but also spiritually significant. Michael Barnes SJ sums this up by asking, 'Can we not speak of Christ as present, if not in the face of the other, then in the *act* of facing?'[12] This way of encountering others does enable us to share some of the profound truths of our faiths, both in the abstract and in the reality of day-to-day life. I came away from those first meetings embarrassed about how anxious I had been and inspired by what had taken place. I couldn't believe that evangelicals had been so reticent to get involved when they were clearly places where truth claims could be articulated, something many evangelicals are concerned to be able to do.

Since then, I have been involved in numerous dialogue events and have learned that some of the most fruitful dialogue comes when we share our own stories and experiences of faith. While there is space for formal conversation about doctrine, it tends to appeal to a relatively small number of people and risks alienating those who are interested in dialogue but feel intimidated by academic topics. However, dialogue that explores a topic such as prayer and invites people to share their practice and experience is much more accessible to people whatever their level of understanding. The Scriptural Reasoning Programme is one model that seeks to do this, described as:

> a tool for inter-faith dialogue whereby people of different faiths come together to read and reflect on their scriptures. Unlike some forms of inter-faith engagement, it is not about seeking agreement but rather exploring the texts and their possible interpretations across faith boundaries, and learning to 'disagree better'.[13]

The dialogue events I first went to worked partly because the meetings created a sense of trust between participants. They weren't a free-for-all or a place where one faith would be challenged more strongly than another; each event was a genuine meeting of equals, which tied in with the second guideline listed above (mutual understanding and trust). This also suggests something different from an informal chat or a fiercely contested debate. In informal conversations people tend to know the etiquette required for them to work smoothly; controversial topics are usually avoided. Good dialogue events, on the other hand, require intentional ways to ensure that there is trust.

In 2009, I and some friends set up the charity The Feast, which applies these principles with teenagers.[14] The events we run are based on good youth-work principles and give young people the opportunity for dialogue between Christians and Muslims. To help the conversations flow and to give the young people confidence, we have developed clear guidelines for dialogue, which we use at every event and which create a safe space for the young people to talk while not shutting down the possibility of profound and challenging discussions. There are ten guidelines. We will:

- listen to what everyone has to say;
- be honest in what we say;
- speak positively of our own faith, rather than negatively of other's;
- respect other people's views, even if I disagree;
- not treat people here as a spokesperson for their faith;
- not tell others what they believe, but will let them tell me;
- acknowledge similarities and differences between our faiths;
- not judge people here by what some people of their faith do;
- not try and force people to agree with our views;
- make every effort to get along with everyone regardless of their faith, gender, race or age.

The guidelines conclude with the instruction that anyone can ask for a discussion to be stopped if they feel uncomfortable. This has hardly ever been used, yet many young people say they like this as it means they can trust the process; they're not going to be asked to say things they don't believe or answer questions they find too difficult. It's a bit like a net round a trampoline: when we had one my son would do all sorts of daring flips and drops as he knew he couldn't fall off, but if he was ever on a trampoline without one he was far more cautious. In the same way the guidelines provide a safety net for the young people, which encourages a deeper exploration of faith.

When people have met and built trust, dialogue can become a way of entering into acts of service together and even the medium for authentic witness, as suggested by the above-mentioned Church of England guidelines. Increasingly, different groups are finding that getting involved in acts of service can actually be the starting point for dialogue. Finding a common cause that people of different faiths can get behind, such as tackling food poverty or caring for asylum seekers, can be the catalyst that brings people together to meet.

Working on the project builds trust, which then creates the space for dialogue. Finding out why people are concerned about an issue can be a great starting point for exploring faith issues about justice, poverty, gender and so forth. The challenge for using service as a starting point for dialogue is that it can stay as a good act of service done by people of different faiths. There's nothing wrong with that, but it isn't dialogue and it might be a missed opportunity to go deeper in understanding and sharing.

Dialogue and evangelism

Dialogue and evangelism are usually considered to be two concepts that don't mix, like oil and water, or that should be kept far apart, like dynamite and matches. This is because typically dialogue is seen as being about building understanding and harmony whereas evangelism is about winning arguments and ultimately souls. If this is the case then, yes, they probably need to be kept apart. But I want to suggest that, rather than being two completely separate concepts, they are actually much more closely linked – and might even be two sides of the same coin.

In the Church of England descriptions of dialogue mentioned at the start of this chapter, the final one is that dialogue becomes the medium for authentic witness. There are many mediums for authentic witness, but dialogue should be seen as one of them. Witness is, of course, not the same as evangelism, but neither is it just about understanding or bridge-building. When we witness to our faith we are giving people an opportunity to form an opinion of it and to have their preconceptions changed or challenged. Dialogue can be a place where we witness by both our words and our deeds; yes, we can explain what we believe and why, but often there is a much more powerful witness in our actions that display our attitude towards others. Being willing to meet, listen to and appreciate the views of others can be a profound testimony, especially for those who feel ostracised by society. We witness to our faith but also to the way our faith inspires us to treat people, to love our neighbours. Linking back to Chapter 1, we can do this only if we no longer see people as being on a spiritual scale. By our actions and words we witness to the way that the Christian faith doesn't define people as good, bad or neutral but as all made in the image of God, with the potential for good in all of us.

Arguably we witness like this all the time in our everyday lives, and others witness to us in the same way. Whenever we encounter someone, we leave them with an impression of us, for good or ill, and we form our opinions of them. In one sense we can't but help witness through dialogue, but the depth of encounter and conversation opens up the potential for authentic rather than superficial witnessing.

However, this isn't evangelism as such. In this context I want to suggest that what makes evangelism different from witness is the intentional hope for conversion in the other. This intention of conversion runs counter to the generally agreed definitions of dialogue. Does this mean, then, that evangelists can't do dialogue? Do they have to pretend to be something they are not if they're to join in?

There are those, such as Paul Knitter, who have argued that evangelists, or evangelicals who have a commitment to evangelism, should not be invited into a dialogue event as they will always want to try to convert people.[15] Their concern is that the approach I've outlined uses dialogue as a smokescreen for evangelism; it's just a way of meeting people in order to try to evangelise them. This argument maintains that the agenda of evangelism will always be present; regardless of what might be said it is always there.

We have to take this concern seriously and make sure that we don't have a hidden agenda. (That's why I'm upfront about my views on evangelism – I can be accused of many things but having a hidden agenda, I hope, isn't one of them!) But agendas shift from situation to situation. When I'm shopping, my aim is not evangelism or dialogue but to get it done as quickly as possible (while trying to be friendly to the shop staff). I don't know what beliefs or ideologies are held by the shop assistants, doctors or bus drivers I meet, as they don't have it on their agendas to tell me; they just get on with doing their jobs. We all operate with a variety of aims and objectives without them being seen as unethical or problematic. In few, if any, other areas do we demand that people give up one of their core beliefs before they can participate. The issue is not that someone coming along to a dialogue event has a calling for evangelism, but rather that they can put that agenda to one side while they participate in the dialogue.

This doesn't mean denying a desire for people to become Christians. In Chapter 4 I described how I answered my Sikh friend when she asked me whether I wanted her to become a Christian. That's the same answer I give in relation to my dialogue work: yes, I long for all people to find the joy, hope and forgiveness I've found through Christ. While I share that where appropriate at a dialogue event, I won't be asking people if they want to consider that for themselves. I might well preach on that in a Sunday service, where people are free to attend or not, or to walk out if they want to.

Dialogue and discipleship

This talk of dialogue sounds lovely and community-minded: having groups of people getting to know one another, sharing their faith and working together is a beautiful image of society. But it can also be naive if it ignores the real differences that exist between us. And just because it sounds good and looks interesting, does that make it a core function of the church? Given everything else we're called to do and the challenge of loving our neighbours and sharing the gospel, do we really have time for this as well? Returning to the idea of the spiritual scale, if we see ourselves as being at one end and people of other faiths at the other, then dialogue probably isn't worth our effort. However, if we are open to exploring the good in them and having our ideas listened to and developed through the encounter with them, then dialogue is not an added extra but a means of exploring the good and inspirational in others while bearing witness to the good news we have to share. It's not an extra activity but an attitude and way of being with others.

In Chapter 1 I showed how people of different faiths can be an inspiration to us, and looked at a number of Bible passages where God's people encountered those who were different and through that encounter were blessed or challenged or transformed. It's easy to assume that this was for the super-holy, the prophets and priests who could cope with being in a challenging multifaith context. But nowhere in the Bible does it suggest that encountering people of different faiths is only for the experts. Sadly, it's become like that in the UK, professionalised so that many non-experts feel that they can't get involved. I speak as someone who has made a living out of this world and can be accused of what I'm bemoaning. That's partly why I'm writing this book, to encourage all Christians to get involved. In my defence, I was no expert when I started; any reading or study that I've done has come about as a result of meeting people of different faiths, not in order to go and do it.

One of the examples I took encouragement from then, and urge others to look to as well, is that of Jesus and his disciples. From the start, discipleship meant following Jesus into some uncomfortable places to meet all sorts of people whom one didn't usually mix with. In Matthew, Jesus calls the first disciples at the end of Chapter 4. Chapters 5, 6 and 7 are the sermon on the mount, so the first extended activity we see is in Chapter 8. In that chapter they meet a man with leprosy, a Roman centurion Jesus describes as having great faith and two demon-possessed men, as well as being caught up in a violent storm that Jesus calms with a word. It doesn't get much easier for them in the next couple of chapters. At the start of Chapter 9 they are at a party with tax collectors and 'sinners' (as discussed earlier in this chapter), and then at the start of Chapter 10 they are sent to drive out evil spirits and to heal every disease and sickness. All this comes right at the start of their discipleship, within the first few months. I wonder what discipleship programmes your church runs for new converts; how closely do they follow this pattern? The point is that Jesus didn't wait until they'd been his followers for a few years before he took them to where they would encounter people very different from themselves; it was from day one. Being a disciple of Jesus means going and being with people different from ourselves, sometimes to serve them, at other times to socialise with them and on other occasions to be inspired or challenged by them, but they are definitely involved.

When viewed like this, dialogue is not a specialist activity or theological discipline but an outworking of the commands to love God and to love our neighbour. As the disciples followed Jesus, they were challenged in their attitudes to neighbours different from themselves; then the encounters drew them closer to Jesus and they retreated for teaching and prayer before going out again. And so the cycle continued – loving God and loving neighbour. If we are going to help people to be effective disciples in a multifaith society, then the solution isn't to hide them away until they're fully prepared but to equip them for these encounters from day one, to grow with Jesus in and through the encounters, not separately from them.

Questions

- How do you see the relationship between dialogue and evangelism? Can someone do both?

- In what ways could you build trust with people of different faiths so that you can have more effective dialogue?

- What is your agenda for getting involved in dialogue? How would you articulate that to others?

6

Being peacemakers

It was a huge crowd that gathered on the side of the hill. The new rabbi was preaching and was incredibly popular. His teaching seemed new and fresh, and it really challenged some of the older teachers. The crowd settled down as he began to speak. They listened to stories, parables, words of wisdom, exhortations and words that comforted, challenged and provoked. No one knew at the time just how important the rabbi's words would be; but that talk, the sermon on the side of a hill, was discussed and passed on for months, years – even centuries.

At the start of what became known as the sermon on the mount, in the famous beatitudes (Matthew 5:3–12), Jesus names those who are blessed. These statements are given as an outline of discipleship, not to describe eight separate groups of disciples; these are the qualities of the same group of people. Furthermore, this is not a description of some elite group of super-disciples more holy and righteous than anyone else but a description of what every Christian ought to be.[16] Within the description of general discipleship comes this famous phrase that speaks into our discussion on dialogue: 'Blessed are the peacemakers, for they will be called children of God' (Matthew 5:9).

Peacemaking all around us

We live in a world where the news would have us believe there is less and less peace and fewer peacemakers, especially among religious people. At times it can seem overwhelming, when news programmes and social-media feeds are full of stories of violence perpetrated in the name of religion, even affecting areas of the world that we've come to assume will be peaceful. Coming out of a police briefing on issues relating to the prevention of violent extremism, I was talking to a Hindu friend who despondently asked if what we were doing was all a waste of time. The challenges seemed so difficult and overwhelming that getting together for dialogue between different faiths in Birmingham all seemed a bit pathetic. There are times when I'm tempted to share his despondency – are we all just having cups of tea together while outside the world is going to hell in a handcart?

While today we are aware of issues from across the globe, no doubt people in Jesus' day could have felt equally powerless in the face of the overwhelming might and power of the Roman empire. What does it mean to be a peacemaker when all around you the authorities can pretty much do what they like? Surely, this is just naive wishful thinking. Yet Jesus clearly expected his followers to be peacemakers and that this was something that they were to be blessed for. Peacemaking is a fundamental part of discipleship, as it reflects the work of God the Father, who brings peace and reconciliation between people and between people and himself. This is why peacemakers are called sons of God, because they are emulating the work of their heavenly Father. Peacemaking is not an optional extra for Christians; it is part of discipleship for all of Christ's followers. This is also a part of discipleship that demands activity; you have to intentionally *do* something to be a peacemaker. The other beatitudes refer to things that happen to people or attitudes that people have, but this is a calling to be active. We are called to be peacemakers not just peace-supporters.

So how does Christ's command to be peacemakers impact the church here in the UK? While we might hear about religiously motivated violence, on the whole most of us live mainly in peace with our neighbours of different faiths. Is peacemaking something that we leave to governments, international peacekeepers and our prayers on a Sunday, or does it have a more immediate relevance for our lives here in the UK?

When the Bible talks about peace, and the way Jesus uses it in this context, it is not just the absence of violence but the deep sense of being *at peace* with those around us. This is not something that happens easily or quickly but is much needed in our society today. This is a peace that we can make in our local communities even if we can't make it across the whole world. As I said to my Hindu friend as we left that police briefing, it might feel overwhelming when we consider the global or national context but we can make a difference in our local communities for the people who live all around us; we can be peacemakers.

Peacemaking all the time

This attitude of peacemaking requires us to be committed to it all the time, as a natural, ongoing part of discipleship. Building peace after conflict is possible, but it's really difficult, which is why so many people are committed to conflict resolution and it has become a significant discipline in its own right. However, building strong relationships when life is generally peaceful is a way of making peace that can sustain communities through difficult times and is a task that everyone can participate in.

Sadly, lots of communities made up of different faiths live at peace largely because people ignore each other. I see this all the time in Birmingham. There is a great acceptance of different faiths in the city and we have people living here from just about every faith and every tradition within those faiths. Not only do we have a huge variety of Christians, from Serbian Orthodox to Caribbean Pentecostal; we also have Sunni and Shia Muslims, Orthodox and Progressive Jews, several different strands of Hinduism and Sikhism, and about ten different schools of Buddhism. Alongside this diversity, there is ethnic and cultural diversity within those faiths, including an endlessly fascinating and complex mix of people. Although there is acceptance of these different groups and some mixing between them, there is also a recognition that many of these groups rarely have meaningful contact with people from a different faith or culture. There is peace, but it is born out of a tolerance of others that largely just ignores them. While this doesn't cause problems most of the time, it doesn't enrich those communities; neither does it build strong relationships to ensure peace in difficult times.

Having a commitment to building peace in Jesus' way is not a soft option that seeks to avoid difficulty, but rather sees dealing with difficult issues as fundamental to peace-building. In my work with young people of different faiths, I've constantly said to them that part of our task is to learn to disagree peacefully. Too many people think that building peace means avoiding controversial topics or areas of real disagreement, when this just delays conflict as eventually those issues will come to the fore and then people lack the relationships or skills to deal with them. Learning to disagree well is a fundamental part of building peace.

Being able to disagree in this way is best done in the context of friendship, as there is then a motivation to avoid insults or aggression as we seek to maintain the friendship despite differences. A Christian once asked me, 'When do you tell Muslims they're wrong in their beliefs?' 'Are you married?' I asked in return. When the man said he was, I asked how long had he been married before he told his wife she that was wrong. Judging by his response I don't think he had done so yet! I don't blame him – telling people they're wrong is difficult, and rarely the best way to get them to change their minds. But asking a spouse or long-term friend why they have a certain point of view and then offering a different perspective is possible; it is not always easy, but is much easier than with someone you don't know.

This principle applies to disagreements with people of other faiths: it's so much easier when you know them. The one comment I dread when I'm meeting someone from another faith for the first time is 'We all believe the same really.' I'm always caught in a dilemma between wanting to be friendly but at the same time wanting to be honest about the fact that there are beliefs that we don't agree on. Having that conversation is much easier with my Muslim, Hindu, Sikh or Buddhist friends than with someone I've just met.

Conflict often comes about when we become suspicious or fearful of people we live alongside. These fears and concerns usually come from ignorance, which is a breeding ground for rumours that can turn people against each other about a false or exaggerated problem. Sadly, there are many examples of conflicts where neighbours have turned against each other with terrifying consequences, whether in Syria, the Balkans or South Sudan; but we also see it closer to home in communities suspicious of those we don't know who appear different from us.

In 2016 Britain voted in a referendum to leave the European Union, for what became known as Brexit. In the days and weeks that followed, police forces and organisations working to counter hate crime across the country reported a huge spike in racist incidents. People who had been living alongside each other, tolerating each other for years, suddenly felt it was okay to shout racist abuse or commit acts of violence. Muslims and Eastern Europeans in particular were targeted. Having been neighbours was not enough to ensure peace. Before and after the vote, we needed peacemakers committed to building deep, lasting relationships. In Birmingham the response to these attacks was a campaign that used the slogan 'Love Your Neighbour'. It started as a collaboration between the church and the Humanist Association and soon drew in different faith communities, civic leaders and people from business and the arts. It wasn't enough merely to look on in despair; the situation needed peacemakers to step in and do something.

Whether we look at serious conflict areas or tensions between communities here in the UK, the lesson is the same: being neighbours does not guarantee peace; what is needed are peacemakers.

Peacemaking and dialogue

This is where the discipleship and the practice of dialogue overlap. Dialogue programmes that are run well and work on building trust create the opportunity to meet, build friendships and explore those things that we find strange, uncomfortable or challenging in the beliefs, practices or lifestyles of other people. However, this is a slow process and requires those involved to stick at it.

We've recently run a series of dialogues called The Birmingham Conversations, which include people of all faiths and none and explore issues affecting people living in Birmingham. We deliberately set out to create a space to discuss issues often considered too difficult for groups to discuss, such as conversion, religion in the workplace and censorship. People commit to coming once a month for six months, with each session lasting three hours. It's a huge commitment and a lot of time is given to building understanding and trust. Even with a committed group who know what they're coming to, it's usually session five before we get real depth of discussion. It takes a long time, but when we do, people open up and share really big concerns and issues. We are then able to explore those and even make recommendations to people with authority about how to address them. This, in a small way, leads to peace between individuals and communities. People have had their misconceptions corrected, have had their concerns taken seriously, have understood the issues facing other communities and have formed friendships across faith or culture.

Peacemaking and evangelism

I recently had discussions with groups of church leaders about tensions they find in ministry among people of different faiths. In every group a few people talked about the tension between evangelism and good, peaceful community relations. The suggestion was that we could either be at peace with our neighbours or seek to evangelise them, but we couldn't do both. As was discussed in Chapter 4, evangelism can be divisive and it is understandable why people consider it to be contrary to peacemaking. Jesus knew that people would reject him and his followers and that following him could cause serious division and persecution (see Matthew 10:16–39).

It's important to note, however, that the persecution comes because of Jesus not because of us: 'You will be hated by everyone because of me' (v. 22a) and 'Do not suppose that I have come to bring peace to the earth. I did not come to bring peace, but a sword' (v. 34). It's very easy to be hated because we behave badly, ignorantly or stupidly, but that is not what Jesus is talking about. Part of the reason for developing the Ethical Guidelines for Witness (see pages 58–59) was to ensure that our behaviour in evangelism was exemplary. We might be hated because of the message and the person of Jesus, but we can make sure it isn't because of our crass behaviour. By thinking about ethical evangelism and ensuring that we constantly put the lessons of loving our neighbour, sharing our faith and being peacemakers together, it is possible to bring together evangelism and peacebuilding. The message of Jesus is bound to offend some and cause division, but our task is to strive for peace even with those offended by the good news of the gospel.

Peacemaking as a lifelong discipline

I know little about horticulture – at home I have only a small garden – but I do know that an oak tree takes a lot longer to grow than a daffodil. And while a daffodil looks lovely it doesn't last as long as an oak tree and can't survive a storm or a cold winter like an oak tree can. If we're going to be peacemakers we need to have in our minds that we want to build peace that's like an oak tree – long-lasting and resilient even in the face of storms – but such peace takes a long time to grow. There are a lot of initiatives to build peace between people of different faiths that come and go quickly. Sometimes they produce good publicity and are visible and media-friendly. They are good but can be a bit like daffodils, lovely while they are there but soon gone. We shouldn't avoid them and they're often worth supporting. But alongside those, the task for Christians is to go on being peacemakers, committed in the long term to seeking peace with neighbours of different faiths, peace that doesn't break down at the first sign of trouble but is resilient, long-lasting and meaningful.

As disciples called to love our neighbours and be peacemakers, being willing to sit with, and listen to, neighbours of other faiths is vital. In this way neighbours become friends, and difficult topics can be discussed. Moreover, because we do this as God's children, we have spiritual resources to draw on to sustain us when things are tough. Peacemaking in this way is long and difficult, and we will often feel as if we are banging our head against a wall. Many a time I have felt like I'm getting somewhere in building strong relationships with Muslim, Sikh or Hindu friends only for them to move away, change jobs or lose interest in interfaith engagement, and we have to start all over again. There are also those who do not want to see peace between communities and will seek to cause division and tension whenever possible, whether these are far-right racist groups, anti-Semitic people or those who use religion to peddle hatred of others. Part of our calling to be peacemakers also means standing up against this hatred. Being a peacemaker means seeking peace for all and not just for ourselves. Jonathan Sacks makes a strong case for Jews, Muslims and Christians to take a lead in challenging hatred done in the name of religion and working together with people of all faiths to build peaceful societies.[17] It's an urgent task for us all.

The risk of not doing this is that, at best, we carry on living in societies where people live parallel lives, walking on opposite sides of the street, ignoring one another. This easily leads to fear and suspicion that breeds prejudice, antagonism and even violence; it certainly doesn't lead to the kind of peace God desires for us.

In Jeremiah 29, we read the letter that Jeremiah wrote to the exiles in Babylon, instructing them on how they were to live in a land where they didn't feel at home, where they were struggling to 'sing the Lord's song', as we discussed in the Introduction. In Babylon they would have been surrounded by the Babylonians eating different food, talking a different language and worshipping foreign gods. We are perhaps most familiar with the stories of Daniel, Shadrach, Meshach and Abednego, who stood firm, faced persecution and came through the ordeal in dramatic and exciting ways. It's easy to think that that is the only pattern God has set for our lives among people of different faiths and cultures. But the letter that we read in Jeremiah 29, which was for the whole community, has a very different message. Rather than urge them into the fiery furnace or den of lions, the Lord tells the exiles to 'build houses and settle down; plant gardens and eat what they produce' (v. 5). Further on he instructs them to 'seek the peace and prosperity of the city to which I have carried you into exile. Pray to the Lord for it, because if it prospers, you too will prosper' (v. 7). Even when they were feeling small and vulnerable among people different from themselves, God's command is for peace. Building peace is not just a luxury for when we have nothing else to do or something we can lead on from a position of strength; God's desire for the world that people should live in peace and that his people should be at the forefront of seeking peace.

Sadly, in Birmingham we've seen the importance of this; fortunately, we've also witnessed what happens when people work to build peace. In 2014 a news story broke alleging that a group of Muslims were trying to infiltrate Birmingham schools in order to impose a strict interpretation of Islam. What became known as Trojan Horse dominated both local and national news for months and caused huge anger and upset among many people caught up in it. Accusations were made against Muslims, Christians, teachers, the local authority and government ministers, to name just a few. It threatened to derail lots of good work done to build relationships between communities and individuals of different faiths.

Yet it didn't, partly because of the people who had committed themselves to the kind of peacemaking I have described. Along with many others, I spent time with friends, and we committed ourselves to that friendship whatever the outcome of the various enquiries that took place. It took huge amounts of time and was a very painful year, yet the peacemaking we had engaged in during the months and years beforehand paid off. Building peace in the good times meant we could sustain that peace in the tough times. This is something we keep on doing, developing strong friendships, building peace now as it might be harder or desperately needed in the future.

In another part of Birmingham occurrences of knife crime and shootings have risen in the past few years. An initiative has started whereby churches walk and pray for peace every month. This has led to practical actions, such as weapons amnesties and knife bins, reducing the number of weapons on the streets. Furthermore, as people have seen the lead Christians have taken, Sikhs and Muslims from the area have started to join in with the prayer walks and are working together to tackle this most serious issue.

Often when we think of being Christians among people of different faiths our default mode is to think about evangelism, dialogue or social-action projects, but it's clear from scripture that another important task for Christians in this area is peacemaking. This is not done as a reaction to violence or conflict but as a proactive task that reduces the chance of conflict, creates relationships capable of enduring difficult times and builds communities of peace for all.

Questions

- Which groups of people live near you whom you rarely meet?

- What could you do to start meeting them (e.g. talk to shopkeepers or go to Eid events)?

- What would your neighbourhood look like if your church sought to fulfil Jeremiah 29?

7

Cultural issues

The preacher walked through the city. He had a few days to spare before his friends rejoined him, so he did what he always did – he started preaching to anyone who would listen. A group of philosophers became interested in his arguments and brought him to speak at their meeting. The beliefs and ideas he was explaining were new to them and they wanted to try to understand this new thinking. The preacher stood up and commended them for being very religious; he had been struck by how many objects were being worshipped across the city. He pointed out to them the way people in their culture worshipped so many things that there was even an altar to an unknown god. 'Let me tell you about this God you don't know,' he said. He then preached a sermon that started with their cultural practices and included a quote from one of their own poets.

Faith, culture or just what we do?

When we think about encountering people of different faiths we often get fixated on their religion, forgetting that they are people with a culture, a family and all the likes and dislikes, hopes and fears that we all share. Understanding their faith and how we relate to that part of their life is important, but if we are going really to love them as our neighbours we need to be interested in the whole of their lives and not just their faith. In the account above of Paul in Athens (from Acts 17:16–34), Paul engages with the Athenian philosophers not just theologically but also culturally. He identifies issues in their culture and then uses these as a starting point for talking about the Christian faith. This is Paul putting into practice what he teaches when he says, 'I have become all things to all people so that by all possible means I might save some' (1 Corinthians 9:22).

Trying to separate religion and culture is notoriously difficult, some would say impossible, as they are often completely intertwined. Being vegetarian might seem like a cultural issue, but for many Sikhs and Hindus it's a significant part of their faith. Dressing modestly could be seen as a lifestyle choice or as an adherence to Islamic teaching on how men and women should dress. When some European countries seek to legislate on the wearing of religious items in public, often the dilemma comes when an item of clothing is seen by some as cultural and others as religious. For example, some commentators see the full-face veil as a cultural expression of Islam, yet for many Muslim women it is an intrinsic part of their faith. It is both cultural and religious, and consequently deciding on whether it can or can't be worn becomes very emotive.

Cultural issues also often cause more tensions in day-to-day life than theological ones, whether it's the right to wear a burka or – the most problematic – parking. I was once at a meeting of interfaith advisors at Lambeth Palace when I said that we could solve all the religious tensions in the UK if we could sort out parking. Everyone laughed and then said, 'Yes, fair point.' Time and again I hear the complaint that during Friday prayers roads are blocked, people park their cars across others' driveways and that it's a nightmare on the roads. I also hear this about gurdwaras on a Sunday, when there's a special occasion like Diwali or if there's a wedding. Whatever the occasion, how people behave in their cars and in relation to others around them becomes a huge source of conflict. Although the issue arises near a place of worship and during services or festivals, it is fundamentally cultural and personal: it reflects people's attitudes towards public space. But, some Christians say, surely their faith teaches them to be considerate of others, and this isn't considerate. That is certainly an issue, but if your culture has brought you up to consider this to be an acceptable way to park, it might be thought of as considerate within a certain cultural view of public space. I know of increasing numbers of mosques who urge their congregations to park considerately, and who sometimes take firm action with those who cause problems for others.

While we can't always separate culture and religion, there are areas of life where we can and it's important to be able to recognise whether we are questioning or affirming a cultural practice or an aspect of someone's faith. This is another reason why living with the blinkers of a spiritual scale can be so damaging for our relationships with others. We might have lots of differences with what someone believes theologically, but find great richness in their cultural practices. I disagree with my Sikh friends about the incarnation of Jesus, but I love their culture of sharing food. Similarly, we might consider someone's faith to be enriching but be appalled by some of the culture surrounding it; for example, female genital mutilation is appalling regardless of what we think of the faith or other cultural practices of people who commit this act.

It starts with us

Before we can critique or reflect on other cultures, however, we need to be ready and willing to do so about our own, which is a much more difficult task. Because culture is the way we live and interact with other people, stepping outside and observing it is notoriously hard. We often need someone else to critique it for us – the good and the bad. As Marshall McLuhan once said, 'We don't know who discovered water, but we know it wasn't the fish.'

Starting the process of engaging with culture means recognising that we have distinctive cultural practices. This might seem obvious but it is amazing how it can be assumed that we are neutral and that everyone else has a culture. In some supermarkets there are aisles of 'ethnic food', as if being white British is somehow not an ethnic category. The implication is that 'they' have cultural food, 'we' just have food. Also, we need to recognise that our cultural practices may or may not be linked to our faith; for example, the way we celebrate Christmas is almost entirely cultural (mostly based on 19th-century ideas). Christians from other parts of the world celebrate Christmas, Easter and the other festivals in vastly different ways, and on different dates. These practices inform and are inspired by our faith, but the fact that we celebrate the birth of Jesus in December with trees, presents and nativity scenes is a reflection of culture.

We also have lots of cultural practices born out of where we live, where we were born, our socio-economic status, ethnicity and so on. These may or may not seem to have much to do with our faith but they will affect the way we behave and relate to other people. I get frustrated when people push to the front rather than queue; this is as much a reflection of my cultural practice as theirs. It's important to say at this point that we need to be careful not to replace the 'spiritual scale' with a 'cultural scale' which says my culture is good and the culture of others is bad. Each culture has good and bad elements to it, but it is easy to assume that because ours feels right to us that it's the best there is. Familiarity does not equal superiority.

Where we might differ

Trying to explore differences between cultures is fraught with problems, as whatever one describes can be challenged by a specific example of someone who does not conform to the cultural description. Undertaking a task like this inevitably draws on generalisations, and needs to be seen in that way. What I am going to describe are things I've found to be generally different between my culture as a white male British Christian and the culture of the Muslim, Sikh, Hindu or Christian friends whose heritage is from the Indian subcontinent. I'm aware that these, like all cultures, are changing, which is something I'll address later in the chapter.

Me, myself and I

There has been lots of discussion in the last few years about the increasing individualism in the West – how, as a culture, we increasingly function as individuals rather than as corporate groups. Adverts appeal to each of us to make our own choices and we are offered increasing individual choice in every aspect of life, from bank accounts to cups of coffee. We even hear it in churches, and I think particularly in evangelical churches, with a strong emphasis on individual salvation and making personal choices about faith. I heard a preacher recently calling people forward to commit to going deeper in their own walk with Jesus. 'Don't worry about the people on either side of you,' he said as a way of encouraging people to respond. 'It's your own choice, not theirs.' Whether this individualism is good or bad is not the point here – it's probably a bit of both. The fact is that for many white British Christians this is the culture that we live in. We speak and act accordingly both inside and outside church. It can lead to the freedom to make choices at odds with those of the people around us but also to real selfishness.

In contrast to this individualistic approach, many of my friends of Asian heritage have a much more communal culture. Decisions are made together; socialising is done within the extended family; people are involved in each other's lives, whether in all going to the airport to meet someone or being involved in choosing marriage partners for people. A friend of mine from a Sikh background once told me that when someone asked him if he wanted to become a Christian it was the first decision he had made on his own. Decisions, even relatively small ones like buying a new table, are family activities. When I ran holiday clubs for children from a Pakistani Muslim background, I learned to encourage them to invite their families, rather than just their parents, to 'show and tell' on the last day, and we changed our expectations of who might come – everybody! I'm also conscious of how strange it sounds to people from these backgrounds if I talk of faith only in terms of my faith and my decisions. I increasingly talk about the faith of my family or the church rather than just my own.

Where are the boundaries?

One of the biggest differences between Asian and white British culture that I encounter is in relation to boundaries. British people, on the whole, like to have clear boundaries for almost everything. Here is my house clearly marked by fences or hedges. My time is clearly marked, so I want meetings to start and finish on time and the time I spend with you will have a fairly clear start and finish, even if that's unspoken. I can also clearly define my family and who's invited to family occasions. Life has clearly defined boundaries.

Many of my Asian friends, however, have a more fluid approach to life. Houses are open to lots of people and the borders are flexible, so people can park all over the place. Time expands and contracts and events start and finish according to their own rules, but rarely bearing any relation to printed start or finish times. Time with a friend will extend over many hours and might include meals, meetings with other people and family time. The boundaries between friendship, work and family are much more blurred. Family occasions become large gatherings of all sorts of extended family and far-flung relations. This difference between clear and fluid boundaries isn't often identified, yet it causes much tension and confusion. It partly explains the tensions over parking when one group wants driveways clearly marked and respected and the other sees the whole road as a short-stay car park. It can feel awkward when we've arranged to meet someone for lunch thinking it'll be for an hour or so, and several hours later there's no sign of the meeting ending.

I encounter the clash between clear boundaries and fluid ones all the time, whether it's a work meeting with an Asian friend that lasts at least three hours and includes lunch in a local restaurant or accepting an invitation to a religious festival as part of my work and finding the organisers are hoping that my family will go as well. Explaining why I have to leave a meeting after three hours or why I've come alone is part of negotiating different cultures. It can be awkward, but recognising it as a cultural clash rather than rudeness or religious conflict helps to keep it in perspective. It also helps me reflect on my culture and on which parts I'm happy to be flexible with or adopt a different approach to.

There is, however, an area of life where having clear or fluid boundaries is often reversed. When it comes to the way the different genders mix, Asian culture often has rigid boundaries whereas Western culture is fluid. Physical contact between genders, including shaking hands, is discouraged for some people, including certain Muslims, some Orthodox Jews and Buddhist monks. I'm happy to shake hands with almost anyone, but if I'm not sure how the other person feels then I smile and say hello to women and wait for them to offer to shake my hand. On the whole that seems to work, but a smile and a sincere apology does sort out most of these situations. This sort of awkwardness is not confined to engaging with other cultures: lots of white British people will greet others with a kiss or a hug, a practice I find awkward and embarrassing unless it's with good friends or family – I'd always prefer to shake hands with people I don't know so well.

I'm the victim

One of the more depressing aspects of my job as the Bishop of Birmingham's Interfaith Director is encountering people who persistently see themselves and their community as victims in every situation. This is an aspect of British culture that seems to transcend faith, ethnicity, gender, age or almost any other category I can think of. I'm constantly talking to people of different faiths who are keen to impress on me why they are the biggest victims of all. It's an attitude that becomes debilitating, with people unwilling to see others as potential victims or to explore ways to move into more constructive attitudes, and it seriously affects the way that Christians relate to people of different faiths.

I'm not trying to play down the seriousness of such issues as racism, sexism, anti-Semitism and Islamophobia. The victims of such abuse need to be supported. What I'm referring to is is an attitude that I describe with the following two sentences: 'I'm the only victim' and 'I'm always the victim'. It's when people fall into believing these two sentences that they become debilitating and unhelpful. If we believe we are always victims, we will never recognise when we are the ones victimising others. If we believe we are the only victims, we won't stand up for others when they are victims.

Islamophobia and anti-Semitism are currently on the rise in the UK. If as a church we are to speak out and stand up against them we have to recognise that we are not the victims in this instance. We also need to examine our speech and actions to make sure that we are not guilty of either of these sins. This is where loving our neighbour becomes a practical, and possibly political, activity. It becomes the inspiration to move beyond seeing ourselves as always and the only victims and gives us the impetus to get involved in the plight of others. If we genuinely love our Muslim and Jewish neighbours, we will be concerned about and seek to act against Islamophobia and anti-Semitism. It's also part of our ongoing task of peacemaking; making peace isn't just for 'our community' but for all people.

Rabbi Mark Schneier in the US is doing a lot of work in mobilising Jewish people to tackle Islamophobia through the organisation the Foundation for Ethnic Understanding. He argues that as people of faith we have to champion not just rights for our community but, more importantly, the rights of others. This is a radical way of challenging the notions that we are always the victims and the only victims. It encourages the community to recognise when others are genuinely victims and to act on their behalf.

As I said, this attitude is prevalent among almost every cultural group I encounter. It leads to fear of others, a lack of interest in their suffering and a self-centred seeking of sympathy and reparation. As Christians, we need to challenge this within our churches and when we encounter it in other people. Highlighting the suffering of people not present can often be a way of challenging the victim mentality of those we are speaking to without trying to manipulate the situation so that we become the real victims.

Class

Britain is often caricatured as, and criticised for, being obsessed with class. We intrinsically know if we're middle class, working class or aristocracy and have grown up with an understanding of that and an ability to identify where others sit within this spectrum. While it's easy to criticise this it's also important to recognise its pervasive influence on us and the way we relate to others, including those of different faiths. In 2015 research was undertaken into children's and adults' friendships, looking at if and how people formed friendships with those different from themselves. The researchers looked at friendships in three primary schools in diverse communities in inner-city London. There is much that is useful in the report but one theme comes out time and again: 'Adult friendships were, like those of the children, more likely to cross ethnic difference than to cross class difference.'[18]

What has often been overlooked in discussions about building friendships with people of different faiths is how much class affects the friendships that are formed. In working-class neighbourhoods, the issue for churches that have predominantly middle-class congregations is, as one church leader put it to me, getting middle-class Christians to make friends with white working-class people, let alone working-class Asians. Class isn't always a problem; there is a rapidly growing Asian middle class and there are many working-class Christians building friendships with working-class Asians, and of course there are those who can bridge this divide. But the reality is that many churches in our inner cities are predominantly middle class trying to reach out to working-class people of other faiths. Recognising the class issue and developing ways to cross this divide is vital if we are to show authentic, unconditional love to our neighbours not just of other faiths but also of a different class.

Expectations of friendship

So far in this book I've argued that one of the great challenges for us as Christians is to love our neighbours of different faiths. For many people this is best expressed by forming friendships. But even these can get tricky. For all the reasons listed above, friendships across cultures can feel frustrating, as they don't always work as we expect.

I was chatting to a Christian couple recently who were experiencing this. On a number of occasions they had invited different Asian neighbours round for an evening meal. This is how they show their friendship, but their neighbours either never accepted the invitation or never invited them back. As they saw it, their friendship was being rejected. Furthermore, the wife explained how she had got to know a Muslim woman well, but had never met her husband. She found this difficult, as it seemed that the woman was embarrassed by her. We talked about different expectations of friendship and the way that activities we assume are normal, such as inviting someone round for a meal, are deeply cultural and might seem intimidating to others. Similarly, we might expect to get to know a wife and a husband, whereas for others it's the norm to become close friends with one and not the other.

I know a number of Asian people of a variety of faiths whom I would describe as friends. We see each other often, talk about all manner of things, laugh together and support each other when things are difficult. But almost without exception we haven't visited each other's homes; I don't know their spouses and we often meet at functions rather than informally. These are friendships that mean a lot to me but are, in many ways, radically different from the types of friendships I have with my middle-class white friends. I've had to learn that friendship can mean very different things, but that doesn't make it less meaningful.

I also know of Muslims who have tried to make friends with white British people, whether Christian or secular, and found their approaches rebuffed. A Muslim friend of mine, after reading the draft of this chapter, told me of how he had recently joined a school governing body and was the only non-white person on the board. He had tried repeatedly to get to know and befriend others on the board to no avail and felt rejected by others who kept to their own friendship groups. It's easy to assume that the way friendships are expressed is universal, but I've learned over the years that the way we live out our friendships is deeply embedded within our culture. What seems like a simple act of friendship can require an awareness of our own cultural expectations and that of others and a willingness to bend and adapt. I've also learned that it's worth talking about these things, helping our friends understand what we both mean by friendship and how we can find ways to express that friendship with which we're both happy. This might mean adapting our expectations or behaviour and, hopefully, finding that understanding and compromise on both sides enrich and deepen our friendships.

Honour and shame

The Asian community is often described as living in an 'honour and shame culture'. Becoming aware of this culture is often an eye-opener for white British Christians, as it can appear very different from their own culture and can explain some behaviour patterns that cannot be simply explained by understanding religious beliefs or practices.

Any attempt to describe this culture has to recognise that, along with other cultures, it is complex and dynamic, shifting, adapting and changing, as seen in the book *Generation M*, which documents the aspirations and ideas of young professional Muslims.[19] What the book's author, Shelina Janmohamed, describes as characteristic of cosmopolitan, business-minded, young, independent Muslims is very different from other people for whom attachment to family and the local community is paramount.

In 2006 the academic Sangeeta Soni wrote an article on encountering honour in Asian communities, particularly looking at its impact on young people and youth work. Along with many other writers, she uses the term *izzat*, which is the Urdu word for honour and one that is commonly used, and points out that this is not limited to any one religion but is evidenced in Christian, Hindu, Muslim and Sikh families. She argues that '*Izzat* is important for Asians because it is a force or phenomenon which confers status on individuals and their families. It sustains a family's good name, standing and reputation within the Asian community.' In other words *izzat* is important, as it directly impacts issues such as your employability or marriage prospects. The more honour you have, the better standing and reputation your family will have. As Sangeeta goes on to say, 'A good position in the hierarchy of families that is established over time is considered advantageous because it ensures that members of that family find themselves in positions of relative privilege.'[20]

While *izzat* affects many areas of life, it particularly affects relationships between men and women and can be used to pass on a moral code often inspired by religious teaching. The Sikh academic Jagbir Jutti-Johal states that for Sikhs 'A fundamental, if not the most fundamental, cultural concept that ensures these religious values [marriage, monogamy and family] are adhered to today is *izzat* (honour) which corresponds with ones standing within the community'. *Izzat* is not just a social phenomenon but is linked to religion, even if it isn't a formal part of any religion and exists in all faith communities. As Jagbir goes on to explain, 'Although the concept of *izzat* is rooted in cultural tradition, it is quite often merged by the Sikh community into the religious tradition, as happens with other South Asian communities.'[21]

This is where the concept of *izzat* can be a powerful force for good across the faiths. It continues to provide a context for passing on faith, culture and a moral code in ways that many outside this culture fail to do. The desire of the community to do good leads to many acts of kindness towards neighbours and strangers, which is regularly commented on by white British Christians encountering this culture for the first time. Being offered gifts of food and entire meals by Muslims during Ramadan or at Eid is a common experience for many Christians. I've been struck many times in recent years by the generosity of many Muslims, Sikhs and Hindus towards the plight of others outside their community. I know of several Muslim groups who, on hearing of homes being flooded in other parts of the UK, mobilised a number of people from their community and went to help clean up and repair the damage, often involving young people so the message of doing good was passed on. Many Muslims I've spoken to about this explain that it is their faith which inspires them to do good, but the way that good is worked out sometimes comes from this culture of honour, which is why it is expressed differently from the way others might seek to do good works. This presents a great opportunity to work together to improve a local area or to fundraise for bigger projects. There have been many occasions in Birmingham when Christians have worked with neighbours of different faiths to support a food bank, clean up litter or fundraise for a national charity.

The flip side to *izzat* is shame. Shame reduces the standing and reputation of the family and has practical implications, just as *izzat* does. It is more than feeling embarrassed or annoyed by someone else's words or actions; the family feel shamed and know that others will see them as having been shamed too. Like *izzat*, shame affects whole families. And just as honour is gained when people see someone doing good, so shame is particularly acute when people are caught acting shamefully. This idea that it's okay to break the rules as long as you don't get caught is, of course, prevalent in all cultures and isn't limited to honour and shame. When I was at school, 'getting away with it' if you broke one of the rules was a badge of honour.

Sadly, this culture of honour and shame is for many people primarily associated with the crime described as honour killing; many commentators (usually white British people) have said that this is the wrong name for it as there is no honour in killing. While I agree with them that it's first and foremost plain murder, the phrase 'honour killing' doesn't mean that killing is honourable but explains the motive behind the killing. Some families get so trapped in a spiral of shame, believed to have been brought on by an errant daughter (and it is almost without exception daughters), that they think the only way to restore honour is to take the most drastic step of killing the daughter. This doesn't justify or minimise the awfulness of the crime but explains what's going on in a situation that most of us find unimaginable.

Honour and shame culture has many positives that commentators often overlook but that are important to affirm. The culture, at its best, provides stability and security for individuals and families. It provides a clear moral and ethical framework that is passed on within families and communities without the need for formal instruction and is part of everyday life. The culture affirms the role of elders and encourages respect for and the care of elderly relatives. It also provides a network for finding marriage partners, employment and financial support along with a strong sense of community, belonging and identity. No doubt there are many other positives, and also ways in which these positive attributes get abused. However, the important thing is that we learn to understand it and look for both the positive and negative attributes in both the honour and shame and guilt and innocence cultures.

As we build friendships with people of different faiths, the critical point to remember is that their behaviour will be influenced by their culture as much as by their faith (just as ours is). Loving our neighbours unconditionally requires us to be willing to understand not just their faith but also their culture and to be willing to see the good in it and not think it is there just to be critiqued. Because cultures are constantly changing – with, it seems, ever-increasing speed – we need to learn the culture of the people we meet and not just presume we know it.

Culture and the Bible

Understanding the culture of others and relating to it isn't a new idea but one that we see in scripture. Right from the outset, God equipped the church to reach out in ways that related to the culture of those around them. When the Holy Spirit came upon the disciples, the first thing they did was to speak in languages that those around them could understand (Acts 2:1–13). They crossed cultural boundaries and engaged with people on their terms. This is an important principle, embedded at the birth of the church, and it comes not as a result of the disciples' trying to work out how to be relevant to the people around them, but by their being filled by the Holy Spirit. In other words, crossing cultures is not a burden or mission strategy, but a move of God between people from different backgrounds. The disciples weren't weakened in their faith through this experience. And neither are the other languages presented as being in any way inferior; rather, they are seen as cultures through which God's word can be spoken and encountered.

Later in Acts we see Peter being deeply challenged about his willingness to encounter people from a different culture. In Chapter 10 he is summoned by Cornelius, a God-fearing Gentile. Peter has to have his attitude towards Gentiles challenged by God through a vision of food coming down from heaven, including food he considered unclean because of his religious upbringing. God makes it clear to Peter that nothing, and no one, is to be considered unclean but that all are equally acceptable to God. It can be argued that this passage shows Peter's prejudices; in verse 34 it's almost as though he's surprised by the realisation that God doesn't show favouritism. Peter is being taught that his upbringing has led him to treat others as inferior because of their race, but that is now being completely overturned through his vision and subsequent encounter with Cornelius.

Scripture doesn't just reach out uncritically to different cultures; it also speaks into and critiques them (including our own, whatever culture we're from). Jesus challenged the culture of public displays of faith, teaching his disciples to perform their religious acts discreetly, to pray in private, to fast without others knowing and to perform good deeds in such a way that only God knows about them (Matthew 6:1–18). This isn't to prove that his followers were more pious or holy than others, but it lifted the burden of keeping up an appearance of religiosity and refocussed them on to a relationship with God.

Sometimes it seems like we make all the running on crossing cultures and reaching out to others. At these times it's easy to feel resentful and consider giving up on the idea of friendships with people of different faiths and cultures. Sometimes we have to recognise that, yes, we do make most of the running. The church has, quite rightly, invested a lot of time and energy encouraging Christians to make friends with people of different faiths. We've produced resources, courses and videos to inspire and equip people and have produced a clear biblical mandate for doing this. We have been able to do this partly because, unlike many other faiths in the UK, we have the capacity. We have also had the luxury to spend time on this as we have not had other battles and distractions that many other communities face. Most of us have not had to fight against racism directed towards us or for the right to build a place of worship or express our faith in public by what we wear or eat. Consequently, we have been able to take a lead on reaching out to others. It is encouraging that increasing numbers of people of different faiths are also now grappling with these questions with a real desire to find effective ways to help people build friendships across ethnic, religious and class divides. It means that we can move to a situation where we can work together on issues such as these rather than feel as if one group has to make all the effort.

Questions

- Try describing the way you practise your faith. How much of what you do is theological and how much is cultural?

- When you meet people of different faiths, what is it in their culture that inspires or irritates you?

- What do you expect a friendship to look like? How might that differ from expectations your Hindu, Sikh or Muslim friend might have?

- How could your church increase its engagement with people of a different social class?

8

The church: reaching out and welcoming in

It wasn't every day that the disciple had a vision of God speaking directly to him, so he knew that on this day something special would happen. He heard God call his name and waited expectantly for a word from the Lord. It started well: 'Go,' came the voice of God. 'I'm ready,' thought the disciple, 'no doubt I'm about to be sent out to preach to the nations, to kings and rulers.' Then God's voice carried on: 'Go to Judas' house on Straight Street.' Well, that was a bit of a come down. Pop round to Judas' house; that's hardly going to change the world, is it? The disciple was getting decidedly unimpressed with this message from God, but it was about to get a whole lot worse. 'There you will find a man from Tarsus praying. He's had a vision that you will restore his sight.' The disciple froze. He knew who had just come and he didn't want to meet him. This was the man who hated the followers of Jesus, a religious fanatic who used religion as an excuse for extreme violence. Why should he go and meet him, and what on earth was he doing at Judas' house? 'I'm not sure that's a good idea,' he said, then instantly regretted it. 'Go!' came God's command again. 'This man is going to take my name to Gentiles and kings and before the people of Israel.' The disciple sighed. Okay, so maybe this might involve kings and significant work for God, but did he really have to welcome that man, could he really have changed? He got up, pulled on his coat and with a quick prayer headed off to Judas' house.

Having considered our attitudes to people of different faiths, some different approaches to how we might live out our faith through evangelism or dialogue, and the cultural issues that can cause division, I want to end by asking what this means for churches and their engagement with people of other faiths. One of my aims in this book is to show that encountering, befriending and sharing faith with Sikhs, Hindus, Muslims and others is not a job just for professional interfaith workers or cross-cultural missionaries. It is a task for the whole church, for leaders and congregations, young and old. It does not require deep study of the beliefs and practices of others, or an encyclopedic understanding of Christianity, but a willingness to follow Jesus wherever he leads and whoever he leads us to meet. Sometimes we'll meet the kindest, friendliest people; other times we'll encounter people opposed to Jesus and the Christian faith. The account from Acts 9:10–17 of the conversion of Saul, retold above, reminds us that God calls people from all backgrounds to follow him. Being willing to welcome them, whatever we've heard or however we feel, is the calling God gives to the church.

What sort of journey?

If, as a church, we are hoping and praying that many people of different faiths will want to become followers of Jesus, then we have to consider what sort of journey of faith we are looking for.

Much literature and training for evangelism assumes that the people we're speaking to are secular and that we start with questions about whether there is a god or not. Clearly this isn't the starting point for people who do believe there is a god; they don't start further back or forward but from a different place. To challenge again the spiritual scale idea explored at the start of this book, we are not moving them from spiritually bad, through neutral to spiritually good. There will be beliefs and practices that need challenging and transforming to be in line with the gospel, as there are for all of us. But there will also be practices and possibly beliefs that are consistent with the gospel, which we can affirm and possibly learn from but which we wouldn't want them to turn away from.

Conversion is often couched in terms of moving from darkness to light, and illustrations of repentance are used that suggest turning away completely from a former life of spiritual darkness to embrace a new one of spiritual light. Beverly Gaventa helpfully highlights different ways that people came to faith in Jesus in the New Testament and makes the point that for many of the people who encountered Jesus there wasn't a complete rejection of their beliefs and faith but a new understanding and realisation of these in the light of Jesus. They didn't stop believing in God but encountered him in a new way; they didn't stop looking for the Messiah but realised the Messiah was going to be radically different from the descriptions they were used to. Even Paul did not reject all his beliefs and practices from before his dramatic conversion, but had them refocussed following his encounter with Jesus. This pattern of reconfiguring beliefs and practices in the light of Jesus can be a helpful way to think of the spiritual journey someone might go on when becoming a follower of Jesus. We don't want people to stop believing in God, praying, doing good, caring for their families, and so on, but would want to help them see how these things are transformed when done in the name of Jesus, through the Holy Spirit.[22]

Pushing only a conversion journey where all the past is seen as bad and all the future is seen as good can lead to really negative attitudes towards the community people have come from. I've met many converts who can see no good whatsoever in the faith they have left; they operate completely within the framework of a spiritual scale and as a result can be critical and sometimes dismissive of their families and others of that faith. This in turn can cause tensions with other Christians seeking to make friends with people of that faith. If they've faced persecution and trauma, then this kind of rejection of the previous faith is understandable; when one has given up everything and risked one's life to convert then it is very hard to describe the old faith as anything other than negative, especially at the beginning. I do not want to challenge those converts struggling with the consequences of the decision they've made, or those early on their journey with Christ and trying to make sense of what conversion means. Rather, it is the language and imagery used by those of us working with them, who casually use simplistic ideas of 'good and bad' that give people no option but to define the past in solely negative terms, that needs redressing. Holding a balance of affirmation and challenge from the outset will help new converts see how they can identify things from their past that can be affirmed and enriched through their encounter with Jesus, as well as areas of their lives that have had a negative impact and need rejecting or healing.

This imagery also impacts the way the church views and treats people who have chosen to convert. If we see everything in their past as negative, and ourselves as spiritually sorted, then they will have nothing to offer us, but lots to learn from us. However, if we do away with that idea and look for the good in their culture and beliefs, we can learn from them and they can become a blessing to us. We have good stuff to share but lots to learn, as do they. When we see people not as spiritually bad or as projects that need saving but as fellow disciples, then we journey together – sometimes with us leading the way, sometimes with us following. When we tear down the false spiritual scale then we have a hope of realising the vision in Mathew 8:11 that 'many will come from the east and the west, and will take their places at the feast with Abraham, Isaac and Jacob in the kingdom of heaven'.

Discipleship

How we care for people who choose to follow Jesus by converting from another faith is an important issue for the church and raises a number of key questions, challenges and opportunities. Discipling someone who has chosen to leave another faith means dealing with the pain and hurt that decision has caused their family and friends and the impact that hurt has on the convert. This might mean walking with someone facing rejection or fleeing persecution – both physical and psychological. I have friends who, through deciding to follow

Jesus, have spent years being ostracised by their families and made to feel deeply guilty by what their decision has done to their family – this is really tough stuff. Choosing to become a follower of Jesus is a fantastic decision but also a costly one, and it can be really hurtful for the family and friends of the person. We shouldn't underestimate that or ignore it, but be asking what responsibility we have to care for the family as well as the convert. They probably won't want anything to do with us, but we can pray for them and seek ways to show them that they are also cared for and loved by God.

Discipleship means growing as a follower of Jesus, which will include reading the Bible, prayer and worshipping with other Christians. Helping people to do this in ways that make sense to their culture and don't require them to adopt all of our cultural practices is vital if we are to help people live out their Christian faith within their own culture and with their own integrity. This might mean putting them in touch with Christians from a similar background or who speak the same language. Fortunately, there are an increasing number of organisations producing resources to help with this task.[23]

However, many churches are finding that discipling people from another faith background can also mean dealing with other complex issues, whether finding them somewhere (safe) to live, helping them find work, managing visa complications or issues for other family members either here or in their country of origin. I was recently speaking to a vicar who is supporting a new convert whose family is in prison and facing physical torture in his home country; the church has been lobbying for their release and raising money to help with legal costs in the country. Other churches are finding that supporting converts means something as fundamental as providing food and clothing.[24]

When we face complex needs like these, being a body of Christ is crucial, because the knowledge, time and pastoral skill required to provide effective care for such needs are often more than one person can handle. We also need to be conscious of the burden this can place on members of the church, in terms of time, ability and emotional and spiritual energy. Another vicar I was talking to recently told me that she has several converts in her church who were imprisoned and tortured in their home country. Members of the congregation wanted to be genuinely friendly and welcoming, but found themselves in situations where the new converts were talking about their traumatic experiences. This left the congregation members deeply upset and not knowing how to respond. They also needed caring for if they were going to be able to listen to and process some horrific accounts of persecution, something completely outside their experience and understanding.

Back to the boundaries

It's often been said that churches in the West aren't very good at welcoming people from different faiths, as all we offer is one service a week and maybe a midweek Bible study for people used to a close community. Solutions to this therefore often involve more church activities. But I think that what many converts are used to, and are looking for, is the unbounded family life that is open and available 24/7. To be a full part of a family dropping in unannounced, sometimes with other friends, staying till late and being part of family celebrations is what has been lost. Most Muslims I know spend little time at the mosque, and while some Sikhs are at the gurdwara for many hours a week often this is for *seva*, acts of service such as cooking or cleaning with a large group of friends and family members. I'm not sure many people are looking for more meetings or more time in church but to be part of a community. For people used to having clear boundaries in life this culture clash can be difficult. Maybe if we are going effectively to welcome and disciple people of different faiths we need to have our boundaries challenged and see it as a joyful task for the whole church to participate in.

Farmers or gardeners?

In Matthew 13:1–23 Jesus tells his disciples the parable of the sower, a great story, which is often acted out (its potential for a large cast of thorns, birds and corn ensures that even the youngest children can have a starring role). As always with Jesus' parables, as well as being entertaining, the story of the sower teaches and challenges us and invites constant rereading to discover new truths. The first thing that I want to point out is that it is the story of a farmer who is sowing seed in order to reap a large harvest. His aim is to have a field of corn, not just one or two stalks. I wonder whether too often we settle for being gardeners rather than farmers. A gardener (apart from the hugely wealthy ones) deals with individual or small groups of plants. They tend them and care for them, but the task is about nurturing small numbers. As I talk to churches I often hear people talking about mission in this kind of language, about working with individuals and seeing one or two come to faith. It's as if we've become content with gardening, caring deeply for one or two, but not seeking huge fields of harvest as farmers do. Yet that is the image in this parable.

This parable is most often used in terms of evangelism, which is hardly surprising given Jesus' explanation. However, I'd like to suggest that the image of a farmer seeking fields of harvest is applicable to all areas of church ministry, whether evangelism, social action, dialogue or the other many and varied church activities that take place. All of these can be done with the outlook of a gardener who treats people purely as individuals and is content with engaging one or two, or they can be undertaken with the attitude of a farmer who sees the individuals but works for whole communities to be impacted. The question it raises is whether we have the vision to see 'fields of harvest' – God at work across communities and many people – or whether we are content with the image of a gardener caring for just a few?

Looking at the parable in this way challenges the individualism of Western culture and makes more sense in the corporate, extended family culture of many Asian people. The main thing to say is that this isn't just an extra project or course that adds yet more committees and meetings to church life; it's an attitude, a way of being. It means we have to change from looking out and seeing just individuals to seeing individuals in communities. This isn't about ignoring individual identity but rather seeing individuals as members of families, communities and faiths with all the complex web of relationships these entail. The plants in a field are all individual but grow close together. Whether our passion is for evangelism, social action, community cohesion or any other area of Christian ministry, the challenge is to embrace this notion of seeing and working with people within, and part of, their communities.

Team work

While one farmer can sow an entire field, it works so much better if there's a team, if the whole family joins in with the work. If we are going to minister to whole communities we need people to meet with parents of young children, teenagers, the elderly, business people, women, men, carers and so on. This would be impossible for one person or even a small committee but becomes possible when the whole church catches this vision. This has the added benefit of challenging the view we have of church; we are not just individuals who meet for worship (and more meetings) but an interconnected family – a body even (1 Corinthians 12:12–31).

For some churches, all this will mean is making new connections between the people engaged in the different activities already happening, stopping to find out which families people belong to. It might be that the mum who brings her child to the stay-and-play is related to the people who helped organise the litter pick and that her sister-in-law is related to the man who spoke at the dialogue meeting a few weeks ago. Suddenly, we can see the mum as an individual who is connected to a much wider group, some of whom we also know already. In this way, the church starts connecting in a holistic way, reaching out to communities through individual relationships.

For other churches this represents a huge challenge – to have the faith, and confidence, to believe that God longs for fields of harvest, and not just one or two plants, and that he calls us to have a vision as big as that. It can seem daunting to a small church, but despite what I just said about working together, the parable is about one farmer. A small workforce, working with God to produce fields of harvest – it is possible.

New relationships

The hope of working like this is that, while it is long term and deeply relational, it has the potential to break down so many barriers between churches and the communities around them. However loving, caring and patient we are, there will be times when we come into tension or conflict with those around us, whether because of conversion, parking, public displays of faith, access to council resources or the many other niggles of life that upset things. For too many churches, the first time they have a conversation with a gurdwara, synagogue or mosque is when there's a problem, which is the hardest way to start. Dealing with conflict or tension is so much easier if you know each other and it's easier still if we know a number of people from the community who consider us friends. It means we know who are the best people to talk to in order to get things done and who the people are who are influential in the community. It also works the other way; people know more of us – and who the really useful people are!

Gradually, we stop being two communities living apart from each other, but friends and neighbours living side by side. It doesn't stop difficulties, but it gives us new means to overcome them. I can talk about conversion with my Muslim friends because we are friends; I can discuss contentious issues about caste with Hindu friends because of the friendship we have. The friendship can survive robust differences if we are committed to that friendship. If more than just one or two people are building these friendships but entire congregations, then we will see barriers breaking down and God, through us, impacting whole communities. We move from being gardeners to farmers.

Not just a waste of time

The final and very encouraging thing to note about this parable is that three out of four areas where the farmer sowed seeds produced no harvest. Sometimes it can feel like we struggle on with no sign of any harvest; we're sowing seeds but nothing's happening. That doesn't mean we're a failure – 75% of this farmer's efforts came to nothing and for the other 25% he had to wait until harvest to see if they would produce fruit. Yet Jesus didn't call him a bad farmer; he described what it's like sowing God's word – hard work. Jesus knew that not everyone would respond to his word; even at the ascension some of his disciples still doubted (Matthew 28:17). Our task is to be faithful farmers, keeping to the vision of fields of harvest and trusting God to grow the seed planted in people's lives.

For some of us this is, perhaps, the biggest challenge. We want to know the outcome of our labours now. We want to be able to share exciting stories of God at work in people's lives and so we want clear answers quickly. But this isn't how God usually works. He grows his word in people's lives; he doesn't forcibly insert it fully formed. This parable challenges us to have the vision for large harvests and the patience to trust that God will bring fruit from some of our efforts.

The challenge of using the parable in this way is that we can be tempted to see our friends and neighbours of different faiths as little more than projects, or trophies to be won. This parable has to be read in the light of the rest of scripture. Yes, we are called to share God's word, but we are still called to love our neighbours unconditionally. This way of seeing the world, as a place where we continually sow God's word and pray for fields of harvest, does not stop if some people reject the message of Jesus or show little interest in our social action or dialogue, and neither does our love for them. I remember once being told very forcefully that this love-your-neighbour stuff is all very well, but shouldn't we be preaching the gospel? My response was that I didn't realise that the two were separate.

We share God's word, sow the seeds, *because* we love our neighbours not *instead* of loving them, and therefore we go on loving our neighbours and loving God however they respond to our words, deeds and witness.

Questions

- Which image best describes your church's attitude to the community around them, gardeners or farmers?

- What would a vision for your church to reach not just dozens but hundreds or thousands of people look like?

- What would your church need to do to become more welcoming to people of different faiths and better equipped to disciple them?

Notes

1 Andrew Smith, *My Friend Imran* (Grove Booklets, 2009), p. 10.
2 Harold Netland, *Encountering Religious Pluralism: The challenge to Christian faith and mission* (IVP, 2001); John Hick, *God Has Many Names* (Macmillan, 1980).
3 James Jones, *Servant* (BLT, 1988), p. 13.
4 H. Clark Pinnock, *A Wideness in God's Mercy* (Zondervan, 1992), p. 29.
5 Gerald R. McDermott, *Can Evangelicals Learn from World Religions?* (IVP, 2000), p. 79.
6 Ray Gaston, *A Heart Broken Open* (Wild Goose, 2009), p. 68.
7 Anil Bahnot, *The Advancement of Dharma: A discussion paper for faith leaders* (Hindu Council UK, 2007), p. 8.
8 Tim Green, 'Conversion from Islam to Christianity in Britain', in Steve Bell and Colin Chapman (eds), *Between Naivety and Hostility: Uncovering the best Christian responses to Islam in Britain* (Authentic Media, 2011), p. 106.
9 http://christianmuslimforum.org/downloads/Ethical_Guidelines_for_Witness.pdf
10 Frances Sleap and Omer Sener, *Dialogue Theories* (The Dialogue Society, 2013).
11 *Towards a Theology for Interfaith Dialogue*, second edition (Church House Publishing, 1986), p. 27.
12 Michael Barnes SJ, *Theology and the Dialogue of Religions* (Cambridge University Press, 2002), p. 238. Emphasis in original.
13 www.scripturalreasoning.org
14 www.thefeast.org.uk
15 Paul Knitter, *Jesus and the Other Names* (Orbis Books, 1996).
16 John R.W. Stott, *The Message of the Sermon on the Mount* (IVP, 1978), p. 31.
17 Jonathan Sacks, *Not in God's Name: Confronting religious violence* (Hodder, 2015).
18 Carol Vincent, Sarah Neal and Humera Iqbal, *Friendship and Diversity: Children's and adults' friendships across social class and ethnic difference* (UCL, ESRC and The University of Surrey, 2015), p. 21.

19 Shelina Janmohamed, *Generation M: Young Muslims changing the world* (I.B. Taurus, 2016).

20 Sangeeta Soni, 'Encountering "izzat" in Asian communities: A reflection on youth work practice', *Youth & Policy* 90 (Winter 2006), pp. 5–17.

21 Jagbir Jutti-Johal, *Sikhism Today* (Continuum, 2011), p. 67.

22 Beverly Gaventa, *From Darkness to Light: Aspects of conversion in the New Testament* (Fortress Press, 1986).

23 See, for example: C. Rasiah and Robin Thomson (eds), *Notes for the Journey: Following Jesus, staying South Asian* (South Asian Concern, 2011); The South Asian Forum of the Evangelical Alliance, *Jesus through Asian Eyes* (The Good Book Company, 2014); and www.joiningthefamily.org.

24 That was the experience of Revd Sally Smith in Stoke-on-Trent: Nazia Parveen, '"This is what I'm meant to be doing": the vicar welcoming Muslims to church', *The Guardian*, 18 July 2016, www.theguardian.com/world/2016/jul/18/this-is-what-im-meant-to-be-doing-the-vicar-welcoming-muslims-to-church.